Jus Humanitatis

The Right of Humankind as Foundation for International Law

Valentin Tomberg

Jus Humanitatis

⊕

The Right
of Humankind as
Foundation
for International Law

Angelico Press

First published in German as
Die Grundlagen des Völkerrechts as Menschheitsrecht
© Verlag Götz Schwippert, Bonn, 1947
First published by Angelico Press, 2023
English translation by Stephen Churchyard
and James Wetmore © Angelico Press, 2023
Introduction © James Wetmore, 2023

For information, address:
Angelico Press
169 Monitor St.
Brooklyn, NY 11222
angelicopress.com

ISBN 978-1-62138-931-6 (pbk)
ISBN 978-1-62138-932-3 (cloth)

Cover Design: Michael Schrauzer

TABLE OF CONTENTS

Introduction i
Overview of Valentin Tomberg's Life i
Tomberg's Works on Jurisprudence & International Law v
A Word on the Title xv

Foreword 1

1. The *Nature* of International Law
as a Right of Humankind
I. Terminology 5
II. Method 8
III. The Worldview Presupposed 20
IV. Presuppositions in the Philosophy of Law 26
V. The Concept, Idea, and Ideal of International
Law as a Right of Humankind 39

2. The *Subject* of International Law
as a Right of Humankind
I. International Law as a *Phenomenon* 48
II. The *Sources* of International Law 54
III. The State as *Subject* of International Law 61
IV. International Law as Law of States and
Right of *Humankind* 72

3. The *Historical Foundations* of
International Law as a Right of Humankind
I. The Historical Beginnings of International Law 107
II. The *Divine-Law* and *Natural-Law* Principles of
International Law, as Known from Historical Facts 110
III. Fundamental Characteristics of the
History of *Positive* International Law 119

4. The *Problems* of International Law Today 150

⊕

This book is dedicated to the memory
of Michael Frensch (1948–2023), leading scholar,
exponent, translator, editor, and publisher of the works
of Valentin Tomberg. His insight and guidance is
present on every page of this edition. He died
just weeks before its publication.

Introduction

Overview of Valentin Tomberg's Life

alentin Tomberg was born in St. Petersburg on February 26, 1900.[1] Baptized a Protestant, he entered the Orthodox church (which he never formally left) shortly before 1933, and, in 1945, became Roman Catholic. His father, Karl Arnold Tomberg, was the administrator of a high school in St. Petersburg, and worked from 1903 onwards as an official in the Russian Ministry of the Interior. After attending St. Peter's School, where he was given a classical education, with teaching conducted in both Russian and German, Valentin studied one semester at the Faculty of Law at the University of St. Petersburg; but the Russian Revolution of November 1917 prevented his further studies. During his life, Tomberg learned to speak fluent Russian, German, French, English, Dutch, and Estonian, and had a good command of Spanish, Polish, Ukrainian, Latin, Greek, and Church Slavonic. In 1918 he fled with his family to Estonia. There his mother, Juliana Umblia, was shot and killed by the Bolsheviks, an event that left deep scars on Tomberg, and shaped his view of communist Russia for the rest of his life. In 1920 he moved to Tallinn, where, between 1928 and 1938, he worked as an interpreter in the postal service administration.

---

[1] According to the Julian calendar then used in Russia the date was February 14th, that is, St. Valentine's day.

In 1925, Tomberg joined the Estonian Anthroposophical Society, becoming its vice-president in 1926 and its president in 1932. From the beginning of the 1930s he began to publish essays in anthroposophical journals. In 1933, he married Maria Belozvetova (1893–1973) in Tallinn, and in the same year his son Alexis (1933–1995) was born. Towards the end of that year there appeared the first of his twelve "Anthroposophical Meditations on the Old Testament"; twelve further such meditations on the New Testament followed between 1935 and 1937. Both sets of essays divided opinion in the Anthroposophical Society, since in them Tomberg developed his own spiritual inquiries, which in part went beyond Rudolf Steiner.[2]

In 1938 Tomberg emigrated to the Netherlands and began actively to lecture on Christological topics.[3] Until the Russian occupation of the Baltic states in 1940, he earned his living as a secretary in the Estonian Vice-Consulate in Amsterdam; thereafter, he was dependent on the support of friends. In the middle of July 1940 he began to teach a weekly course on the Lord's Prayer to this circle of friends.[4]

---

[2] Valentin Tomberg, *Christ and Sophia, Anthroposophic Meditations on the Old Testament, New Testament & Apocalypse* (Great Barrington, 2006).

[3] Two of these lecture series were later published in book form: *Sieben Vorträge über die innere Entwicklung des Menschen* and *Die vier Christusopfer und das Erscheinen des Christus im Ätherischen* (the former was published in English as *Inner Development*, most recently in 1992; the latter, under the title *The Four Sacrifices of Christ*, is contained in the volume mentioned in note 2).

[4] Published by Achamoth Verlag in four volumes as *Der Vaterunser-Kurs* and subsequently in English as *The Course on the Lord's Prayer*. An earlier translation by Robert Powell is available at sophiafoundation.org. A new translation is currently in preparation by Angelico Press.

Introduction

This course, which was organized as a series of meditative exercises affording deep insights into Christian esotericism, was broken off in 1943 because of the threat posed by German occupying forces.

The longer the war went on, the more Tomberg sought to find an organization or community with a Christian basis that had not been corrupted or destroyed by National Socialism. He found it at last in the Catholic Church. Tomberg's trust in this institution rested, first, on its established hierarchy and its seven sacraments, and second, on the fact that a series of Catholic men and women had offered resistance to the Nazis and paid the price by perishing in concentration camps.

At the beginning of 1944, Tomberg moved to Cologne at the invitation of the legal scholar Ernst von Hippel (1895–1984), whose friend he had become. In the same year he was awarded the title of Doctor of Law for his dissertation on "The Degeneration and Regeneration of Jurisprudence."[5] The second work on international law, here published in English for the first time in a readily accessible edition, followed at the beginning of 1945.[6] Tomberg then worked on his *Habilitationsschrift*[7] in the Faculty of Law of the University of Cologne, probably until 1948, which was intended as

---

[5] Published in 1946 by Verlag Götz Schwippert, Bonn. Reprinted in 1974 by Bouvier Verlag, Bonn. Published in English by Angelico Press in 2021 as *The Art of the Good: On the Regeneration of Fallen Justice*.

[6] *Die Grundlagen des Völkerrechts als Menschheitsrecht*. Published in 1947 by Verlag Götz Schwippert, Bonn.

[7] The *Habilitationschrift* is a post-doctoral qualification conferring the *venia legendi* ("right to read," i.e., to lecture) needed before an academic may take up a university professorship.

an outline of a new legal order for post-war Germany. The fate of this text remains unclear: there is some evidence that Tomberg may have destroyed it after realizing that German law and politics were developing in a different direction, and as the partition of Germany by the Allied forces began to look likely. Since he no longer envisaged working as a university lecturer in international law (as he had previously done at the Technical University of Aachen), he moved to England, where he later completed his jurisprudential magnum opus (see below).

The law professor Fritz von Hippel (brother of Tomberg's close friend Ernst) suggested to Tomberg in 1949 that he should write another work on international law. This text was finished only at the end of 1952 and was first published in 2022 (seventy years later!) in the original German under the title *Vom Völkerrecht zur Weltfriedensordnung* [From International Law to World Peace].[8] Thus, Tomberg's four works in the field of jurisprudence were the fruit of a period of activity lasting from 1944 to 1952. More will be said later in this introduction regarding these works and the events of Tomberg's life during which they were composed.

In July 1945 Tomberg, with his wife and son, had moved into a camp for "displaced persons" in Ossendorf, Cologne,

---

[8] The original manuscript was titled *Die Problemgeschichte der Völkerrechtswissenschaft*. The publishing company Herder Verlag had planned an omnibus of articles by various authors on the history of international law, and Fritz von Hippel asked Tomberg whether he would like to contribute to it; but it appears Tomberg misconstrued the inquiry to mean he was being asked to compose an independent work on the subject. Only after completing this task did he learn that Herder had made no such request and would not undertake its publication. Angelico Press is preparing an English translation of this work.

where he worked for the British Army as a translator. In December 1945 the Tomberg family relocated to Mülheim, in the Ruhr region of Germany. In 1946 Tomberg began lecturing at the technical college in Aachen, specializing in ethics and law. There he led the rehabilitation of the adult education center. In 1948, as mentioned before, he moved with his family to London, then a year later to Reading, where he worked until 1960 as a translator for the BBC and continued to write on international law (as well as on religious-spiritual and intellectual-historical topics). In 1952 he became a British citizen. Between the years 1958 and 1967 Tomberg composed the text he is best known for, *Méditations sur les 22 arcanes majeurs du Tarot* (published anonymously),[9] now considered a spiritual classic. His final works, written in German, were published posthumously.[10] He died on February 24, 1973, on the island of Majorca, and was buried in the cemetery in Palma de Majorca.

Tomberg's Works on Jurisprudence & International Law

As stated before, more remains to be said about Tomberg's life and work in the context of this second of his works on true *justice* to be published by Angelico Press, works com-

---

[9] In English, *Meditations on the Tarot: A Journey into Christian Hermeticism*, republished in an expanded edition by Angelico Press in 2020.

[10] Published in 1985 by Verlag Herder Basel as *Lazarus komm heraus! Drei Schriften von Valentin Tomberg*, then in English translation as *Covenant of the Heart* (1992) and again slightly revised as *Lazarus Come Forth!* (2006). A new translation was published in 2022 by Angelico Press in three separate volumes: *Lazarus: The Miracle of Resurrection in World History*; *Proclamation on Sinai: Covenant and Commandments*; and *Thy Kingdom Come: The New Evolution of the Good*.

posed during and in the aftermath of the holocaust of the Second World War. At that time, in which all social and legal order was in a worsening state of collapse, Tomberg nonetheless single-mindedly pursued his legal studies at the University of Cologne, working with determination towards his doctorate. At first sight, it seems hardly credible that such a topic could be chosen and permitted at a university in a totalitarian state—in which, day in and day out, the greatest *injustice* was taking place, and in which Nazi control over the academy had long been a *fait accompli*. But the University of Cologne was an exception in this respect, and by July 1944, Tomberg was already being entrusted by the university's board of trustees with the tasks of an academic assistant in the Institute for International Law. Although work could not then take place at the university itself because of what was happening in the war, Tomberg continued to study at home in Bad Godesberg, close to Bonn.

It was during this time that Tomberg settled upon the theme of "The Degeneration and Regeneration of Jurisprudence" for his dissertation, which was written under unbelievably exacting circumstances. Although Bonn and Bad Godesberg had not previously figured as prime targets in the battle plans of the British and American air forces, all this changed in October, 1944. The Western allies wanted to test a more advanced version of their "radio bombing" system, for which three conditions were needed: a previously undamaged city center, a location on a river, and inclement weather at the time of the attack. The first and second conditions made Bonn an ideal target. And when the third condition was met on October 18, 1944, the old town of Bonn was destroyed. Incredibly, it was immediately after this raid that Tomberg applied to take the oral examination for his doctorate before completing his dissertation. In addition to this, he had enlisted in the emergency services and been called into action on the Siegfried Line, where he contracted pyelitis and cholecystitis.

This dissertation—his first writing on jurisprudence—marks a major turning-point in Tomberg's life. Studies on spiritual-humanistic topics that he had presented during his thirties in anthroposophical terminology are here superseded by a strict orientation towards a Platonic model of knowledge and a medieval, so-called "realism of universals." With the assistance of Goethe's phenomenological method, and reference as well to Rudolf Steiner's approach to epistemology in the latter's seminal work, *Die Philosophie der Freiheit*,[11] Tomberg aims to show that the spiritual or intellectual substance of law is a *reality*. He describes law as an organism consisting of several levels, each of which corresponds to a level of cognition: the *ideal* of law, the *idea* of law, and the *concept* of law (over which latter the two other levels preside). For Tomberg, a correct appreciation of the "positive law in force" (what is obligatory for the actual administration of justice) must rest on the *concept* of law (positive law, *lex positiva*), itself derived from the *idea* of law (natural law, *lex naturalis*), which in turn originates in the *ideal* of law (divine law, *lex divina*).[12]

Philosophical analyses and studies in the history of law convinced Tomberg that the modern path *away* from a nat-

---

[11] Various editions of this work have appeared in English, under the titles *The Philosophy of Spiritual Activity* (Steiner's preferred translation of the title), *The Philosophy of Freedom*, and, more recently, *Intuitive Thinking as a Spiritual Path*.

[12] A fourth traditional level of law, the eternal law (*lex aeterna*), transcends the world, in which it appears only as mirrored by the *lex divina*.

ural law founded upon religion, and *towards* a legal "positivism" oriented towards power, had led to a dismantling of the different levels of law and the loss of both the *idea* and the *ideal* of law. This dismantling he describes as a process of *degeneration.* In Tomberg's dissertation, which reveals him as a Christian humanist thinker, he proposes reorganizing the academic study of law in such a way that access to the higher levels of law (the *idea* of law and the *ideal* of law) might be restored, that is, *regenerated.*

⊕

The subject of Tomberg's dissertation points as well to another turning-point in his life. Whereas he had mainly concentrated during his time in the Netherlands on anthroposophical studies, his attention now turned to the situation of *humankind* as a whole. This extension of Tomberg's field of inquiry brought with it a shift in his orientation towards the "universal church," with its hundreds of millions of members—a church concerned likewise with the affairs of all humankind. Alongside the Orthodox church, Tomberg took the Roman Catholic church to be the most important representative of the "universal church." Indeed, in his dissertation he gave prominence to the Roman Catholic church (referencing its monarchical, aristocratic, and democratic elements) as an example of *true community.* It may even be argued that it was precisely this widening of Tomberg's field of inquiry that led him to questions of law in the first place, for in Tomberg's eyes the human catastrophe of the Second World War was a consequence of the *overthrow* of law by overbearing states intoxicated with their own power: above all, of course, by Bolshevist Russia and Nazi Germany.

This overthrow of law, so opportunistically tolerated by the mass of legal scholars and lawyers (if not actually justified by them!) was not, for Tomberg, something *inexplicable* appearing "out of the blue"; it was, rather, the *inevitable* consequence of the *degeneration* of jurisprudence and the "positive" law founded upon it—a degeneration that had begun in the Medieval controversy between Realism and Nominalism, had continued in the Renaissance and Early Modern period, had led to the European revolutions, and had now culminated in the modern totalitarian state. Moreover, as we have seen, Tomberg was at this stage himself operating in the maw of this degeneration day in and day out in a Cologne more and more devastated by each successive Allied fire-bombing attack. He wished to work against this onslaught in his jurisprudential studies as a means to contribute to a *regeneration* of jurisprudence, and thereby to restore and further the complete hierarchy of law.

⊕

In a central passage of his dissertation, Tomberg cited Leibniz's view regarding the connection between the several levels of law and the levels of human relationship. At the first level, men live and strive for the realization of true happiness through individual perfection; at the second level, they strive for shared perfection as a folk, nation, or state; at the third level, they live as the community of all humankind in communion with God, that is, as a "universal church." What should be carefully noted is that Leibniz's fourth and final goal is *not* that the church (in this "universal" sense) should be absorbed into the state, but that the state should become a church. A "state church" would be the complete opposite of Leibniz's conception. While writing his dissertation, then, what hovered before Tomberg as the goal to be striven for was not the gradual absorption of the church into the state, but the absorption of the state (along with its economic and political special interests) into the church— which would be no other than the realization of St. Augustine's *City of God*.

This unification of different levels, which Tomberg vigorously presented in his dissertation as a feature lying at the core both of being and of knowledge, together with an analogical model of being and of knowledge laid out according to hierarchical levels, was soon to appear as the guiding theme in Tomberg's late work and magnum opus *Meditations on the Tarot: A Journey into Christian Hermeticism*. Leibniz is referred to in that text also, supplemented by an Hermetic exposition of the divine name *Yod-He-Vav-He*, in which each of the four divine letters is assigned its own level of knowledge and particular sense-organ. The "jurisprudential phase" of Tomberg's life can therefore be seen as carrying the seeds of this latter work.

⊕

We turn now in more detail to Tomberg's second jurisprudential work (conceived and in part written at the turn of the year 1944–1945), here published as *Jus Humanitatis: The Right of Humankind as Foundation for International Law*. As in his dissertation, here again Tomberg develops his topic from a spiritually comprehensive worldview.[13] In his dissertation, Tomberg had portrayed the gradual degeneration of jurisprudence against the background of what St. Thomas

[13] We mean by this that in other works written both before and after this present text Tomberg wrote in remarkable detail on the subject of the

Introduction

Aquinas described as the several essential levels of law. And here Tomberg again starts out from the idea of jurisprudence divided into levels—arguing in detail that, in consequence of a protracted process of degeneration (exacerbated by the course of modernity), the higher levels of law are no longer to be found in contemporary legal codes. He shows how the earlier, comprehensive conception of law as developed by Aquinas was gradually collapsed. For Aquinas, the summit of the edifice of law, and also its foundation, is the *lex aeterna* or eternal law (law in *union* with God) that invisibly and irremovably underpins all law, thereby conferring *actual* legality upon every individual statute. This transcendent, eternal law is mirrored in the world as the *lex divina* or divine law. The divine law is mirrored in turn in the world as the *lex naturalis* or natural law (the feeling for law as native to human beings), which in turn establishes in them an orientation that carries through (or that ought to carry through) into a law generated by free human beings amid the actuality of life on earth as the *lex positiva* or "positive law in force." According to Tomberg, however, this latter level in the hierarchy of law runs the risk of degenerating into an anti-legal "power principle," as manifested in totalitarian states.

It is in the context of this lowest level of law in the overall scheme of the hierarchy of law that Tomberg situates his

above-mentioned hierarchical levels of individual, nation, and humankind as a whole from the perspective of the "celestial hierarchies" as portrayed in Christian tradition—and, from among the traditional nine hierarchies, more specifically those of the angels, archangels, and archai (or principalities). More will be said on this subject in the final section of this introduction, "A Word on the Title."

views on the right of humankind as a whole. In Tomberg's religious-spiritual writings, this nadir in the "fall of law" may be seen as analogous to the nadir in the "fall of man" represented by the turning-point of the Passion of Jesus Christ. And it seems likely that just such a correspondence between a turn toward the raising or regeneration of law to the level of *humankind*, and the greater turn—through the crucifixion, resurrection, and ascension of Jesus Christ— toward the regeneration or raising of *humankind*, is what Tomberg had in mind when he chose for the book's title the little-used German word *Menscheitsrecht*: "right of humankind" (or "law of humankind").[14] Although Tomberg did not specifically offer a Latin equivalent for this level of law, we have added to the book's title the Latin expression *jus humanitatis* as a way of situating this further step in the hierarchy of law within the traditional Latin framework of Aquinas, which in fact is still fundamental in jurisprudential teaching today.

⊕

In his fourth book on law, *Die Problemgeschichte der Völkerrechtswissenschaft*,[15] Tomberg presents the *history* of international law in a broader overview, formulating his results in such a way that they are fruitful not only for the special case of the existing constitutional arrangements of a particular nation, but can in principle serve the peaceful coexist-

---

[14] The German *Recht* can mean both "right" and "law." In the compound *Menscheits-recht* its sense is closer to "right," so the term is generally translated as "right of humankind," although when it is a matter of situating *Menscheitsrecht* in the hierarchy of law (divine law, natural law, positive, etc.), it is sometimes rendered also as "law of humankind."

[15] See page iv, fn 8.

ence of *all* nations on earth when governed by *true* reason, *actual* justice, and *lived* humanity. Whereas in his earlier texts on jurisprudence Tomberg had demonstrated the collapse of the ideal of law and of the idea of law (the *lex divina* and the *lex naturalis*) into the positivism of the enforced law (the *lex positiva*) of the modern age, in this, his final, jurisprudential work, he returns to subject of the step-by-step dismantling of the edifice of law. But he presents this now more particularly as the eclipse of the *lex divina* and of the *lex naturalis* in the so-called "law of nations" or *international law*—a process that, according to his analysis, began as a purely methodological exercise but in the end led to the *de facto* eclipse of the higher vocation of international law; indeed, so much so that this vocation came to be understood for all practical purposes (that is, positivistically) as nothing more than a legitimizing of *absolute power*, which then led further (as Tomberg was all too painfully aware)[16] to the final degradation of international law from its true foundation in the right or law of humankind to the absolutely sovereign (i.e., totalitarian) modern state.

⊕

Going a step further, we may say that, with his four studies on jurisprudence (or, perhaps better said, on true justice) and international law, Tomberg built a sort of edifice laid out in a very particular order. Looked at in this way, his first book (his dissertation, *The Art of the Good: On the Regen-*

---

[16] Recalling in particular the murder of his mother by the Bolsheviks, his labors during the Nazi invasion of Holland, during the bombing raids in and around Cologne, and then again for many years monitoring Soviet bloc propaganda broadcasts for the BBC.

eration of Fallen Justice) served as a concise sketch of the path towards making *contact* with the integral essence of law as an ideal or archetype. It depicts the stages by which the edifice of the ideal essence of jurisprudence came to be demolished and forgotten during the course of the history of the West, while also highlighting the need for a turn toward a higher, humanly-regenerated foundation of law. His second book (*Jus Humanitatis: The Right of Human-kind as Foundation for International Law*) served as a guide to the *realization* of this higher, regenerated right or law of humankind that supersedes that of nations or states. It seems that his third book (the so-called *International Law II*, which is lost to us) was intended to have an actual *effect* in a particular historical situation, that of regenerating the substance of a German law that had degenerated and in the end been annihilated in the Nazi period. And finally, his fourth book in the series (*From International Law to World Peace*) may be thought of as a philosophical *summa* of his jurisprudential research and insights.

What emerges for the first time from this arrangement is the fourfold structure (contact, realization, effect, philo-sophical *summa*) that Tomberg would later expound, in the first four "Letters" of his great work, *Meditations on the Tarot: A Journey into Christian Hermeticism*, as the themes of *mysticism* (contact), *gnosis* (realization), *sacred magic* (effect), and *Hermetic philosophy* (philosophical *summa*)—themes whose significance for "total" human knowing and being it was his mission to bring with regenerative clarity to a new generation, itself standing at a critical turning.

A Word on the Title

The deceptively simple-looking German title of the present text, *Die Grundlagen des Völkerrechts als Menschheitsrecht*, calls for close scrutiny. Whereas *Völkerrecht* ("international law") is standard in the usage of German jurisprudence, this is not the case with *Menschheitsrecht* ("right of humankind" or "law of humankind"),[17] which tells us by implication that the related German legal term *Menschenrechte* ("human rights") was not adequate to the perspective Tomberg is at pains to develop here. This point is all the more important in view of the content of Tomberg's broader cultural and Christological writings, where he presents a perspective on jurisprudence of unexampled depth, garnered from the point of view of the spiritual provenance and distribution of law and order (jurisprudence and guiding judgment) as it cascades into our human world from the celestial hierarchies of Christian tradition.[18] For this reason, wherever the expression "right of humankind" or "law of humankind" is met with, the reader should be alert to the special significance nascent in Tomberg's presentation.

Put briefly, Tomberg's jurisprudential views draw upon his deep Christian insights into the teaching of the nine celestial hierarchies. The hierarchy of law as described in these works may be brought into connection with the three lower ranks of the ninefold celestial hierarchy: angels, guiding spirits of *individuals*; archangels, guiding spirits of *peo-*

[17] See page xii, fn 14.
[18] See *The Art of the Good: On the Regeneration of Fallen Justice*; *Proclamation on Sinai: Covenant and Commandments*; *Lazarus: The Miracle of Resurrection in World History*; and *Meditations on the Tarot: A Journey into Christian Hermeticism*.

ples (folk), i.e, nations or states; and archai, guiding spirits of *humankind* for set cycles of time. Looked at this way, we might consider this second of Tomberg's books on jurisprudence as associating the "right of humankind" (or "law of humankind") with the hierarchy of the archai, who exercise their guidance from one rank higher than that of the archangels (who guide individual peoples or nations) and two ranks above the angels (who guide individuals).

MICHAEL FRENSCH
JAMES R WETMORE

Foreword

The present work was essentially conceived, and partly written, at the turn of the year 1944–1945. At the time, four-engined bombers were humming overhead. Almost without interruption, windows and doors were shaking from exploding ordnance nearby, reminding everyone of imminent danger, and thus calling for the serious reflection that is brought on by the proximity of great suffering and death. This study is the result of that seriousness. It is especially intended for readers who, even today, retain that seriousness—that is, who are conscious of their responsibility for the happiness and unhappiness of all *humankind*.

In the author's distant native land of Russia, there is an often-quoted proverb, "When the forest is chopped down, the wood chips fly": that is, when the whole is at stake, no account can be taken of the individual. In most of the countries of Europe, innumerable completely innocent men and women, as well as their children, have had to discover the truth of this proverb all too clearly during the war years. It was the *states* who presumed to embody the highest values —i.e., that they were called to lead humanity—who brought about that war by putting their political schemes into effect. They did this by dragging the heavy roller of their technical and military might over people, presuming, again, to evoke in the survivors the hope that these same states, with their politics of the "balance of power" and their

1

way of "resolving" problems by force of war, would now build a free and just order. But were they *capable* of this?

We, the wood shavings of the felled forest, can hardly do other than doubt this. If the Holy Alliance, founded in the name of God; if the Hague Convention, set up on humanitarian grounds; if the League of Nations, called into life in the name of humanity—if all these proved inadequate to avert the disaster of this last world war, then it is in truth *not* the fault of the Holy Alliance, the Hague Convention, or the League of Nations that this war came about, but simply and solely the fault of the *states* themselves, whose power all these checks on power proved unable to restrain.

Now, the states have had their span of authority. They have had ample opportunity to show whether their "unlimited self-rule" signifies weal or woe for humankind. They have emancipated themselves from all higher obligations (God and the Church now being "private matters" for individuals—i.e., for us wood-shavings), and with all their political resources and power have shown the whole world what they intend with their freedom. If states were to retain the same degree of self-rule into the future, how could we be sure those states would undergo a shift and make quite different and better use of their resources?

⊕

These are the questions that coursed through the author's soul during air-raids, in the bunkers, in the cellars. And since the turn of the year 1944–1945, a great deal more has occurred to place these same questions in the tragic light of the experienced fact that there are still states that have "learned and forgotten nothing." For, if the establishment of the United Nations represented the idea (which followed with iron necessity from the war experience) that the states must be subordinated to a higher authority and that humankind as a whole must be vouchsafed the right of oversight and sanction as regards individual states both in respect of their domestic concerns (no "iron curtains" in the world!) and in that of their foreign policy, and if the movement towards the foundation of a European Federation is an attempt to bring about this same idea in the narrower theater of European relations, there nevertheless stands *against* this idea the process (provoked and caused by the Soviet Union) of the formation of "blocs"—i.e., the very negation of the idea of a "right of humankind" [*jus humanitatis*][1] standing *above* the individual states.

The recently-concluded Moscow conference of the great powers showed once again, with perfect clarity, that the old idol of the absolute sovereignty of the state has *not* been overthrown, but, to the further detriment of humanity, still reigns. It is not the atom bomb that fills us today with the greatest concern, but the *ideology* of the atom bomb—i.e., that power is the "ultima ratio" of the claims of those individual states that persist in wishing to know themselves to be self-governing.

The idol of the states' unlimited self-government must, however, be overthrown. In its place an international law must be brought into effect, a law that is no longer a state law (i.e., a product of self-governing states) but an enforceable right of humankind standing above those states. The right of humankind *trumps* or *supersedes* the law of states. Our aim in the present work is to offer a modest contribution to the grounding, propagation, and realization of this

[1] See Introduction, page xii.

3

truth of experience. It is *dedicated*, however, to all the innocent victims of unlimited state sovereignty across the globe—in particular to the fresh graves of the children of Warsaw, Rotterdam, Belgrade, London, Coventry, Kiev, Odessa, Sebastopol, Cologne, Hamburg, Stuttgart, and dozens of other cities, neighborhoods, and villages in which children have been the victims of "total attacks" from the air—as well as to the mothers of these children.

The Author, Mülheim/Ruhr, May 1947

1

The *Nature* of International Law as a Right of Humankind

The Concept, Idea, and Ideal of International Law

I. Terminology

hat was understood by "international law" until the Second World War was the sum-total of all the legal norms that applied (or ought to have applied) to at least two and at most to all unlimitedly sovereign states, as well as to that branch of jurisprudence whose task it is to explore these norms. The same word thus designated both the science of international law and the object of this science, i.e., the law that governs and obligates states.

However, the fact that, according to the prevailing doctrine, international law applied not to *peoples* but to *states*, occasioned criticism of this description and a series of suggestions for replacing it with a better one. As early as 1650, Zouch suggested that the description *ius gentium*, which had been used by the Romans and whose literal translations were in German *Völkerrecht*, in French *droit des gens*, and in

English *law of nations*, should be replaced by *ius inter gentes*. This expression was subsequently translated into English by Jeremy Bentham as "international law" and introduced into France by Bentham's friend Etienne Dumont as *droit international*. From the French, this expression spread over almost the whole world.[1] Some authors also employ the expression "public international law" (*internationales öffentliche Recht, droit international public, derecho internacional publico, diritto internazionale publico*) with the intention of excluding international private law from the field of the law of nations.

More recently, suggestions have not been lacking as to how a new description for international law might be selected. Franz von Liszt, for example, regards the description *Staatenrecht* ("law of states")[2] as more to the point, since, in his view, international law is concerned only with the legal relations among states. The American commentator Ellery C. Stowell, on the other hand, suggests the term *supra*-national law instead of *inter*-national law.[3] He argues for this on the grounds that since states are only representatives of the interests of individuals, the latter are the real subjects *both* of international law and of law as such. Since, however, the sum-total of individuals is in fact *humankind*,

---

[1] *Derecho internacional* (Spanish); *diritto internazionale* (Italian); *mezhdunarodnoye pravo* (Russian), *internationales Recht* (German). Alongside these descriptions, however, the older ones were also used: *direcho do las gentes* (Spanish); *diritto delle genti* (Italian); while in German and Dutch the old descriptions *Völkerrecht* and *Volkenrecht* are most often used. In Russian, however, this older description does not occur.

[2] Hereafter, *Staatenrecht* will usually be translated as "law of states," for the same reason given above in footnote 1. ED

[3] *International Law* (London: H. Holt, 1931), vii.

it is the right of humankind that binds states and stands *above* them as law. Hence the expression "international law" in the sense of *an authority higher than the state*.

Now, the fact that Lizst and Stowell offered such contrasting suggestions points to something more significant than the question of which technical terminology is to pass current; for the *ideological* opposition between the two authors is revealed in their respective choices of the expressions "law of states" and "supra-national law." While Liszt is concerned to portray the *state* both as the highest subject of law and as the author of law—i.e., as the source of international law—Stowell is concerned to show that, in reality, only human beings can be either subjects or authors of law, and thus that states (and other corporations or bodies) can only be regarded as legal persons or treated as the imaginary subjects of law for so long as, and insofar as, the authority delegated to them by the *people* whom they represent remains valid.

Terminology becomes a weighty matter here, since it has the significance of a *profession* of faith. If by "international law" one wishes to understand either the "law of states" or "supra-national law," one is therewith nailing one's colors to the mast. And so it is only right that we too should nail our colors to the mast by adopting a keyword to express the conception of international law that will underlie the whole of the present study. It is only fitting, after all, that we not rest content with half measures, as Stowell does, but instead follow to its end the path Stowell embarked upon by suggesting the simple but highly significant description "right" or "law" of humankind (*Menschheitsrecht, droit de l'humanité, derecho de la humanidad, pravo chelove-chestvo*, etc.) as a sort of interpretative supplement to "law of nations." It is of course not a matter here of replacing the expression "law of nations" (whose use has been sanctified by the passage of time) with a new expression, but of supplying an *additional* description whose use will be appropriate wherever it is a question of a law that—whether by virtue of its content or because of the domain to which it is applied—relates to humankind.

II. Method

Since international law is the concern of *humankind*, it is bound up in the closest possible way with all of human culture. Like religion and ethics, it belongs organically to the universally human social and cultural legacies, which can certainly be isolated from the whole of human spiritual culture for purposes of theoretical analysis, but can never subsist for themselves alone in actual human practice. Just as the *language* we make use of in expressing the concerns of international law is not some sort of artificial Esperanto, but the living universal language of cultural exchange, so the concepts, ideas, and ideals of international law are nothing other than the concepts, ideas, and ideals of the universal intellectual life of humankind—i.e., of religion, philosophy, and science, applied in a specialized way to a particular field. For this reason, the nature, principles, and foundations of international law cannot be understood or correctly evaluated in their full amplitude within the context of the whole array of cultural values if, in order to be observed and portrayed, they are first ripped from the soil in which they are rooted.

If international law belongs to the legal life of humankind if that legal life may not conflict with reason and ethics (because it is itself guided and shaped by reason and ethics),

8

and if, in their own development, reason and ethics themselves depend upon ideals deriving in the last analysis from religion, then international law can only be a part of the *whole* that embraces law, ethics, philosophy, and religion. Detaching international law from private law (as has happened over the course of the development of Roman and canon law in particular over the last two thousand years); detaching law-as-such from metaphysics (i.e., from philosophy); separating philosophy from ethical life; separating ethical life from religion—these are not stages of progress! They are, rather, stages of impoverishment, a narrowing of the circle within which we frame the problem.

A "de-Romanized" international law; a philosophy of law "purged of metaphysics"; a "moral-free" science; a "de-theologized" philosophy—these characterize the tendencies of the span from the time of the "Enlightenment" to our own. They are manifestations of progress in the sense that time moves on, but not in the sense of any deepening, expansion, or elevation of the corresponding concepts, ideas, and ideals. To the contrary: the preponderant tendency ever since Kant towards a "clean break between different fields" has separated almost all fields from each other—a process that has by now gone so far that professors in two different faculties often have so little to say to one another that for topics of conversation they are reduced to whatever happens to be the latest news of the day. All this is at the cost of a universal spiritual culture: *Wagner*, the research assistant, rises; *Faust*, the doctor, declines.

⊕

Taken to its logical conclusion, this separating tendency devolves into the disintegration—that is, the death—of any

9

real life of the mind. After all, if we do not come to a halt (and why should we?) with separating philosophy from religion, ethics from philosophy, and science from philosophy and ethics, the next step will commence with separating science from logic as such (i.e., from judgments and inferences) and then from abstract concepts of any kind—so that in the end we will be left busying ourselves about a mass of concrete sense perceptions, rather like little children playing at a game!

The absurdity of continuing in this direction beyond even the limit already reached today is obvious. Yet we are still at it, striving in manifold ways to root out all higher values in favor of what lies beneath them. In jurisprudence, for instance, we are not content with having already eradicated the two higher storeys (the ideal and the idea) of the previously three-storeyed edifice of law and natural law, but aspire to eradicate the very *concept* of law, so that we can settle on a "law" lacking any "law-in-itself," that is, a "law" resting upon nothing more than the arbitrary power of those who command whatever state power happens to be considered valid at the moment. The legal proverb *Recht ist, was gilt* ("law is whatever counts as valid")[4] brings to jurisprudential expression a conception of "law" that has given up *law* in favor of *validity*.

Here we have an advanced stage of the separating tendency. Law is first separated from what is true and good in-

---

[4] "It is just as impossible to discover universally valid concepts of the validity of the prescriptions of international law as it is in the case of intra-state law. Here, as there, we are referred to the assertion that 'law is whatever counts as valid.'" (Th. Niemeyer, *Völkerrecht* [Sammlung Göschen, 1923], 39)

itself (i.e., from God). Thus is *divine law* eradicated from consciousness. Next, the echo or reflection of this divine law, accommodated now to suit human reason and ethics (so-called *natural law*) is eradicated. Then, at last, we come to the point where even the concept of law derived from the age of natural law, and still surviving in the legacy of valid, *positive* law, can be eradicated in favor of the foundationless principle that "law is whatever counts as valid."

How would it be if in a similar way we supplanted the concept of truth in philosophy with the proposition that "truth is whatever counts as valid"? It would be the last nail in the coffin of philosophy! It would amount to relinquishing the aim, direction, and criterion of thinking as such. It would signal the end of all philosophical activity.

Now, the case is no different with a jurisprudence that lacks a concept of law: when it relinquishes law-in-itself as its aim, direction, and criterion, it also ceases to be a science, a methodically-cultivated body of knowledge. Just as there can be no mathematics without "number and size," without *quantity*, so there can be no jurisprudence without *law*.

The tendency in science to eradicate the *ideal* in favor of the *phenomenal*, and thereafter to treat the "liberated" remnants as science-in-itself, leads to absurdity. In the present work, therefore, we take the other path: the unification of everything that belongs together by virtue of its *nature*. We treat law as inseparable from *justice*. We treat justice as inseparable from *ethical life*. We treat ethical life, with its ideals and tasks, as inseparable from *religion*.

International law will here be considered in its organic connection with the whole life of law, with ethical life, and with religion. Yes, international law is a particular field of law—but it is a field into which the currents of the total spiritual culture of humanity flow together. It is not separated from the integral life of the spirit, as though a glass sphere surrounding an artificially produced homunculus. The problem of international law that has been presented to us by the catastrophic events of the two world wars is not merely a juridical, political, and economic question. It is a moral and religious question also. It is a *total* question of human culture. And we owe it a *total* answer. We owe it an answer that takes into account the *totality* of the question, an answer that points towards a legal order for humanity that is capable of rescuing human culture (a culture threatened with death), a legal order that is capable of rescuing that culture for the future, of preserving it, of enabling it to develop further.

⊕

The method we must follow, the only possible and permissible method, is an examination that does justice to the *synthetic* (i.e., organic) unity of the life of the spirit—in contradistinction to the *analytic* mode of examination that first separates the whole in order to treat what has been thus artificially sectioned off as though it were a world-unto-itself. To be sure, some degree of *articulation* is necessary in order to examine an object scientifically, but this is a preparatory, provisional procedure, undertaken solely to ensure that in the end the whole can be known—known, not as some indeterminate "cloudy" entity, but as an articulated organism.

Analysis precedes synthesis. It separates the elements to be brought together later. For example, the articulation of the total field of law into private, public, and international law can perform a valuable service. But it can do so only if that articulation is undertaken simply to the theoretical end of clarifying what is unique and individual. If instead, by implication, it entails license to take one field seriously and others not, it becomes harmful. When the goal of analysis is to act in *service* of synthesis, it contributes methodological clarity. But if analysis becomes its *own* goal, it loses any governing criterion. It loses the capacity to situate or orient the inquiry—i.e., the capacity for judgment "adequate" to reality. Analysis is fruitful only when it serves to prepare the way for synthesis. If pursued as an end in itself, it is the death of ideals, ideas, and concepts; it leads to a mental shallowness in face of which the analyst who adopts this sole approach can scarcely be distinguished from a stamp-collector.

⊕

The other hallmark of our method in this study is its relation to the truth content and to the ethical content of ideas. It treats these *contents* as values grounded in and justified by what is of value in them—values whose power of conviction derives from the selfsame source. If a thought is outlined perspicuously enough for its content to appear clearly to the consciousness of an attentive and objectively prepared reader (i.e., by an inference that sets the thought alongside or in contrast to other thoughts by means of illustration through analogy, or by being clearly formulated in words), it is left then to the thought itself to speak and to convince through its own content alone. If the *weight* of the truth content or the ethical content of a thought has made no persuasive impression on us by means of our *immediate* perception of it, no amount of proof or experiential results will suffice to make that impression. The *content* always has

13

the final and decisive word by way of the evidence it provides.

In the end, all proofs, deductions, or appeals to our own or to others' experience have only the significance of offering an *illustration*. They merely serve to assist others in achieving immediate insight into the content of the thought. And only such insight provides unshakable cognitive certainty, i.e., actual knowledge. This is so, because, although knowledge *can* be incomplete, it *cannot* be uncertain. As long as such intuition contains even the least degree of uncertainty, it is not knowledge. It is merely opinion or possibility. All intuitions that do not rest upon immediate insight into the essential content of the object of knowledge, but are instead based on the fragmentary contingencies of external experience, are just such opinions and possibilities. This is why Plato distinguished *three* stages in the emergence of knowledge: "knowledge itself," or immediate insight into the essential content of the object of knowledge (*episteme*); "a most probable possibility," acquired by means of logical connections (*dianoia*); and "opinion," grounded on the fragmentary givens of sense experience mediated by subjective inclination (*doxa*).

The whole process of knowledge thus begins with the stage of the stimulus given by experience to the life of thought. If we remain at this stage, satisfied with subjective opinion, with *doxa*, we are, so to say, of the "rank and file." If we make better use of the stimulus by undertaking a serious intellectual labor of checking and deliberating upon all the logical possibilities it may entail in order to come at last to the "most probable possibility," we have attained the stage of *dianoia*, which immediately precedes *episteme*. In having come thus far (that is, to be resting content with the

14

"most probable possibility of all"), we will have constructed for ourselves a hermeneutic to guide our engagement with the life of knowledge. But even for us as author of this theoretical construct, one day it may collapse because it lacks "total certainty." Total certainty is reached precisely at that stage of the process of knowledge when we raise ourselves *above* the "most probable possibility of all" to an immediate insight into the meaningful moral *content* of this possibility. This qualifies us either to reject this possibility with decisive certainty, or to be convinced of it with decisive certainty. Only *episteme* brings real certainty, i.e., actual knowledge.

Just as we ascend in the process of knowledge from *doxa* (opinion), to *dianoia* (theoretical probability), to *episteme* (immediate insight of essence), so do we descend through the same three stages in *shaping* the knowledge thus acquired. For with knowledge, it is not only a question of its acquisition, but of making what we have acquired of service to others—i.e., of *expressing* this acquired knowledge in such a way that others may come to know in like manner to how we ourselves first came to know it. In shaping the path leading to this further knowledge, we descend by the same steps we previously ascended. In this descent we commence with the pure spiritual and moral content of knowledge, *episteme*, which stands before our consciousness as an *ideal* absolute in its content. Through *dianoia* we then draw all the consequences of this ideal of truth for discursive logical thought. In this way, the ideal becomes the creative and determining center of a whole organism of thinking, that is, an *idea*. Finally, if through *doxa* we are able to bring the ideal further into the realm of a thinking grounded on sense experience in order to show both how it is at work shaping the multiplicity of appearances and how it can be acquired through abstraction from sense experience as a shared characteristic, then the idea becomes a *concept.*

Ideals, ideas, and concepts are the three stages by which acquired knowledge is shaped or given form, just as opinions, possibilities, and insights are the three stages by which knowledge is acquired. In sum, the *immediate content of an insight* is the goal and criterion of the method we will be using.

⊕

The method we are describing is not new, as can already be seen from the supporting example introduced from Plato. On the contrary, it is as old as is thinking humanity itself. In antiquity it was championed by Plato, Aristotle, and their successors. In the Middle Ages it was championed by the Realist tendency in Scholasticism.[5] In the modern era, it appeared under the sign of Idealism. We encounter it again in the realm of jurisprudence and the philosophy of law as the "school of natural law." This current of Realism (in the sense that ideas are realities) has of course undergone many metamorphoses over the millennia and has set various tendencies and schools in motion. One thing, however, has always remained its essential characteristic: insight, or the *seeing of ideas.* And too this has always been opposed the essential Nominalist characteristic: *blindness to ideas.* The Sophists, Cynics, Sceptics, and Epicureans of antiquity, the Nominalists of the Middle Ages, the "empirical" Realists of

---

[5] In opposition to Nominalism, which sees in universal concepts (*universalia*) only verbal signs (*mere voces*) of sensuous experiences. Nominalism, however, was condemned by the Church, and thus Realism prevails even today as the method of Catholic theology and philosophy.

the modern era, and the pure positivism of jurisprudence in the present (all of which were, and are, either completely blind to ideas, or at least very short-sighted towards them) were always opposed by those (for example, Socrates) who possessed the capacity for *insight* into the world of pure content, and who, as witnesses and servants of that world, sought always to guard against humankind wasting away its life of the mind.

Both of these currents are present with us, even though it is the Nominalistic current that has gained the upper hand in science, politics, and economics. This ascendancy of the Nominalistic current is owing to the fact that the techno-logical sciences had no scruples about placing their research and discoveries in service to the destructive ends of waging war. To this are also owed the unscrupulous and impover-ished political ideas of most states, great and small. Finally, the two world wars and a series of bloody revolutions are the consequence of a loosening of the "ideal" constraints that had formerly protected humankind from catastrophes of this kind. If there is no remnant left of the ideal of humanity-in-itself, why should a people not put its own goals and dreams of power in the place of the missing, abso-lutely binding ideal? If there is no heaven in the sense of a value that stands *above* the human being, and if conscience becomes a matter of taste, why should one not think of *soil* instead of heaven, and *blood* instead of conscience as the highest values?[6] Or again, if there are no higher spiritual values, there can be neither a social hierarchy nor a hierar-chically-structured Church. And so, the call is: let every-thing arrayed above us be torn down; let the rabble hold

---

[6] An allusion the National Socialist ideology of *Blut und Boden*. ED

sway! National Socialism and Bolshevism, with their millions of victims, are consequences of the contemporary dominance of Nominalism, i.e., of the rule of those for whom thinking is nothing more than a technique for realizing pragmatic goals.

A heavy responsibility weighs upon those who champion a denial of the reality of a revelation of the spiritual. And yet, no change in their attitude, no insight into the nature of the guilt they bear, is to be expected from them. For such a change of attitude, such an insight, already *presupposes* the capacity to see the spiritual and moral connection between their influence on the world and the catastrophic consequences of that influence. Such an insight, however, would only be possible were they actually to become Realists, i.e., were they to receive insight into the moral and spiritual *content* of the meaning of the present series of catastrophes.

⊕

A dispute between the tendencies of Realism and Nominalism (in the sense of some sort of polemic) would be wholly fruitless today. The centuries-long history of this dispute has already shown its hopelessness. Just as at the time of Plato and the Sophists, and during the Medieval dispute over universals, so, even today, the champions of these two tendencies are no less at loggerheads. The reason behind this irreconcilability does not lie in a dearth of argumentation or of eloquence, or in a lack of honest effort, but instead in the fact that the two tendencies actually represent two different groups of people. While the Realist feels the reality of the ideas to be an *effect* fully "adequate" to experience, the Nominalist experiences only a shadow, an insubstantial abstraction. Whereas the Realist, when engaged in thinking, experiences a stream of illuminated revelation from the spiritual world, the Nominalist experiences thinking, not as a window into the world of illuminated content, but instead merely as a categorization of a sum-total of sense experiences. The difference between the two lies precisely in the inner *experience* of the life of the mind. That is why the *difference* between them cannot be removed by discussion, and also why neither the one side nor the other can be convinced by means of arguments.[7]

Above, we described these two qualities as the "seeing of ideas" and "blindness to ideas." We did so precisely because the Nominalist does not experience anything essentially *different* from what the Realist experiences. The *distinction* between them is, rather, that the Nominalist experiences a limited part of what the Realist experiences—that is, the Realist experiences in thinking what the Nominalist experiences... and more besides. There is no *qualitative* distinction between the experiences of the two, then, but only a difference of *degree*. Where the one sees only a shadow, the other sees a living being: but living beings do *also* cast a shadow.

Just as there are musical and unmusical people, so there are people who "see ideas" and people who are "blind to ideas"—with the difference, however, that unmusical people do not presume to guide the development of music, whereas leadership in the field of the cultural sciences is today largely in the hands of people "blind to ideas." Since the cultural sciences (among them jurisprudence in partic-

---

[7] This does not mean to imply that no change of one's attitude is possible, or that one's make-up cannot be changed for the better, only that this cannot happen by means of *argumentation*.

ular) have to do with ideal values, they can and may only be cultivated by those who possess an *organ* for grasping these ideal values. Just as we cannot and may not be a theologian if we deny the existence of God, so we cannot and may not be a jurisprudentialist if we deny the existence of law-in-itself. A jurisprudence without law is quite as impossible as is a theology without God.

In conclusion, it should be said that the method followed here with respect to international law as a law humankind consists in wielding the usual techniques of legal and historical scholarship in such a manner that international law can be understood as an inseparable member of the organism of the whole spiritual culture of humanity, as sharing in its sickness and in its health. Furthermore, this understanding will be a *Realist* understanding, which is to say that its certainty as knowledge will be owed to the *ideal* content of international law.

III. The Worldview Presupposed

Every scientific method presupposes a worldview, whether it does so explicitly or tacitly. Now, since "method" is the way we arrive at a particular goal, it is part of every method, to posit in advance a particular goal (i.e., a value for which we are striving by means of our method) and to find, choose, or create the *means* that will lead us to the goal posited. Neither the positing of the goal nor the choice of the means leading to it is something contingent; both are grounded in, and determined by, the overall conscious disposition of the person in question towards the world. The *direction* we take, and the possibility of *orienting* ourselves in the forest of empirical experience, is not owed to empirical experience itself (otherwise there would be no method, but instead a "being-driven here and there by chance") but to *intuitions* about matters of *principle* that we have acquired for ourselves.

The first beginnings of international law, for example, are usually portrayed in such a way as to suggest that primitive humanity consisted of small clans or tribes conducting wars of extermination against each other—such that entire adversarial tribes, including women, old people, and children, were annihilated. Then, so we are told, there came a time when the realization dawned among humankind that there was an advantage to enslaving adversarial tribes rather than killing them off. And so the war of annihilation became instead a war of theft—more particularly, the theft of persons. With the passage of time, tribes grew in numbers and became peoples; and wars became lengthier and more exhausting. This led to a shift towards *treaties*. At first, such treaties meant that one people was coerced by another (war of subjugation), but later on treaties (as peace treaties) served also as preventative measures against war, which in turn brought with them an increase in *trade*. According to this view, it was in just this way that international law gradually emerged as the law of war and peace—at first among tribes, but later also among *states*.

⊕

It should be noted well that the above portrayal is grounded in a particular methodological presumption: that the direction of movement is from the primitive (or cultural minimum) to the civilized (or cultural maximum). The most bestial point (i.e., the minimum quantity of the human) is taken as starting-point. A line of gradual progress is then

21

traced from this starting-point to the *present* state of civilization (as the given maximum quantity of the human). But this method, let us recall, is rooted in convictions that belong to a particular worldview: the dogma that the past of humankind was more bestial than its present, and that our contemporary situation is the result of *progress*. This historical dogma is based in turn on a corresponding cosmological dogma, namely, that the world, with all its beings and objects, has developed from the simplest primary cells. In other words, what is qualitatively simplest and most imperfect is said to produce, in the course of the world's development, what is qualitatively most complex and perfect—i.e., it is from unconscious matter that consciousness emerges in the world. In short, the qualitative minimum is the source of the qualitative maximum.

It is quite possible, however, to portray the whole process of the emergence of international law in quite another way. We can just as well start out from the principle that bestiality, savagery, and brutality were not the starting-point of an ascending development but the *end-point* of a descending development—i.e., that bestiality, savagery, and brutality represent the final outcome of a process of degeneration and not the initial stage of generation. But think: do not Australian aborigines exist alongside European civilized humanity even today? Did tribes and hordes of savages and half-savages always exist *alongside* high civilizations? The Great Wall of China enclosed a high civilization, yet beyond that wall nomadic tribes of Mongols wandered. Babylon was a flourishing city, yet the Arabian steppes of the time were inhabited by nomads also. And the same goes for Mexico and Peru, ancient India, the Greek colonies, and the Phoenicians. Experience tells us that civilization and primitive peoples[8] always appear in parallel. This is what the historical *facts* teach.

Why then should the "secondary" phenomenon of primitive peoples existing alongside more advanced cultures be awarded priority? In point of logic, the opposite conception is equally tenable. In fact, the cultural traditions of almost all nations concur that once there was a *higher* spiritual state of culture (the *Golden Age* of Greek and Roman tradition, the *Satya Yuga* of Indian tradition), which over the course of time has been *lost*. On what grounds may we dismiss this tradition, rather than accepting it as actually buttressing the logic that points to the possibility of *degeneration*? If we decide in favor of the theory of degeneration, we will be in a position to portray the first beginnings of international law quite otherwise than we did at the outset of this section. For this altered case we would need to speak, rather, of how an *original* human religion—and a mysterious being at the center of this religion—governed the life and commerce of humanity by means of laws and commandments, etc.

It is not a question of taking up a position in favor of one side or the other, but of giving an example of how things *can* be treated differently if we start by presupposing a different worldview. In our present discussion, for instance, the theory of "degeneration" clearly results from principles informed by a particular worldview based upon the principle that a minimal degree of quality can emerge only from a greater degree of quality, and not the other way around. Just as parents precede children, and children can neither be born nor remain alive if parents do not feed and raise them, so, according to this latter view, humankind descended

[8] *Naturvölker.*

23

from and is cared for, accompanied, and taught, by a being *higher* than humankind itself originally was—and does *not* descend from a lower or bestial being.

The same principle might, by analogy, be applied to the world. It also takes its origin from a higher being, God. The world is a creation, a work of consciousness; consciousness is not a work of the world. Consciousness can be *reduced* to the level of a deep sleep (i.e., to matter), but it can never *originate* from matter. What we are illustrating here (the dependence of method on worldview) with reference to *one* example (the portrayal of the first beginnings of international law) could as well be illustrated with reference of many other examples. But to do this would be superfluous. It is not the quantity of examples cited that is decisive; it is, rather, insight into just how a method *depends* for its content on the worldview that underpins it.

⊕

In the field of the cultural sciences there is no such thing as a method unassociated with a worldview, nor could there ever be such a method. The worldview in question may be more or less conscious, or it may be hidden in the unconscious; but either way it never ceases to exert a determinative effect upon the method with which it is associated. For our purposes, however, the presupposed worldview is not meant to remain concealed. Rather, it is to be placed in the brightest possible light at the very beginning of the study. "Scientific objectivity" does not consist in lacking a worldview, but—as required in view of the demands made by an intellectually and morally well-grounded worldview that does justice to the facts—holding our personal sympathies and antipathies in check.

The *Nature* of a Right of Humankind

The fundamental presuppositions of the worldview at work in the present study are the following:

(1) The world is neither a mechanical nor an organic automaton that brings forth blind beings (including, for the purpose of argument, the geniuses of human history) from its dark, subterranean realms. It is a *creation on the part of the highest consciousness.*

(2) The world, as a creation on the part of the highest consciousness (i.e., of God) is not an end in itself. It is a wisely and benevolently appointed stage upon which conscious beings can develop their *freedom.*

(3) The development of the freedom of these conscious beings is expressed especially in the presence of the possibility of their coming into *opposition* with the creator and the creation. *Good* and *evil* are objective realities in the realm of the unfolding freedom of these conscious beings.

(4) All conscious beings are connected by a bond of *fraternity* that they owe to their common origin and their common vocation.

(5) This common vocation of conscious beings is salvation, which can be attained by the use of freedom for good. The misuse of freedom, by contrast, brings about the evil of a state of separation from, and opposition to, the original source of salvation.

(6) On account of the misuse of freedom that took place in the past, evil prevails in the realm of the consciousness and the bodily organization of humankind, alongside the consciousness of salvation and natural health.

(7) The hope of redemption from this state of the human being and of humankind is to be found in the *saving truths* of Christianity, truths that for this reason are the lodestar on the path to overcoming the spiritual, social, and economic ills of the present and of the future.

IV. Presuppositions in the Philosophy of Law

The principles of international law as a right or law of humankind can only be spoken of after we have come to an agreement about the principles of *law in general.* This agreement must be reached in advance of considering particular problems of international law, as an introduction to them—for it represents the necessary connecting link between the presuppositions of our method and worldview on one hand, and the real object of the present study on the other.

The three kinds of knowledge—or, more correctly, the three stages by which we arrive at *certain* knowledge—were discussed above. Drawing on Plato, we called them "opining" (*doxa*), "logical insight into possibility" (*dianoia*), and "immediate insight" (*episteme*).[9] These three kinds of knowledge represent the connecting links between the *moral* and *natural* world-orders. *Doxa* is the result of inferences drawn on the basis of facts perceived by the senses. *Dianoia* covers the middle area of pure thinking in Kant's sense, in which one concept is deduced from another. Finally, *episteme* is an immediate insight into value, which

---

[9] Cf. J. Sauter, *Die philosophischen Grundlagen des Naturrechts* [Philosophical Foundations of Natural Law] (Vienna, 1932), 23–24.

means to say it is grounded in a sense-free, self-evident perception into the moral world-order. It is this immediate insight into value that underpins both jurisprudence and awareness of law as such.

Now, law, which is the basis of all jurisprudence, is *not* an object of sense perception, and so cannot be arrived at empirically. For even if we acquire the *concept* of law from individual phenomena of "law" that come to our notice, these phenomena only come into being in the first place because there already exists in the world a law that reveals itself through them. The *universale post res*, the *concept* acquired by abstraction from the multiplicity of phenomena, owes its coming-into-being in human consciousness to the *universale in rebus*, that is, to the objective reality of the *idea* that reveals itself in those phenomena. The idea truly does reveal itself *in* the appearances as their common shaping principle, but it is not fully revealed all at once: it retains within itself a "remainder" of *as yet* unrealized possibilities of revelation. But an idea that is not completely revealed in the world of things (i.e., of phenomena) is an *ideal*. An ideal is an idea that has taken only partial shape, or no shape at all. It is the *universale ante res*. It is the archetypal element "pre-existing" the idea that reveals itself in things, which for their part precede the concepts acquired of them through abstraction in human consciousness. The concept is the part of the phenomena-shaping idea that has *so far* been received into human consciousness, that is, been conceived by it.[10] The idea is the part of the ideal that has *so far* managed to become manifest. Summarizing:

[10] *Begriff*: "concept"; *begriffen*: "conceived." ED

27

The ideal *precedes* things; it is the *universale ante res*: the archetype of the things concerned.

The idea works creatively *in* things; it is the *universale in rebus*: the forming principle of the things concerned.

The concept emerges *after* things; it is the *universale post res*: the abstraction acquired from things.

As regards the connecting links of the concept, idea, and ideal with the three kinds of *knowledge* we have discussed:

Doxa, the forming of opinions applied to external experience (phenomena, things), raises itself from individual appearances to *concepts*: to the *universalia post res*.

Dianoia, the knowledge of possibility, is able to ascend from the concept to its *idea*, leading consciousness thereby to the reality of the *universalia in rebus*.

Episteme, the immediate insight into value (and it alone) enables consciousness to ascend to immediate intuition of the *ideal*: the *universalia ante res*.

Just as the three stages of knowledge belong together, so also do the three *results* of the three stages of knowledge.

⊕

All this is to say that the *ideal* of law is just as necessary to jurisprudence as are the *idea* of law and the *concept* of law. The *total* reality of the life of law is thus disposed in three stages, as are also both the method of knowledge and knowledge itself. There was a time when everyone was aware that law has three stages. The Medieval Scholasticism of Albertus Magnus and Thomas Aquinas taught law in three stages:

Divine law (*ius divinum, lex divina*)
Natural law (*ius naturae, lex naturalis*)
Positive (or, human) law (*ius humanum, lex positivum*)

Divine law is the ideal of law. It is what gives the life of law a goal and a direction. Natural law is the ordering governance of reason and morality in human collective life. Positive (or, human) law should, by right, constitute the degree of realization of natural and divine law (i.e., of the idea and ideal of law) reasonable or appropriate for any given stage of humankind. In actuality, however, it does not only represent that degree of realization; it also contains statutes that are not an expression of law, but of *power*. Positive law as the sum-total of such statutes brought into force in the course of legislation (the making of laws) is thus a mixed territory in which law, legally insignificant statutes, and outright injustice are in force alongside each other.

⊕

Now, the task of jurisprudence consists precisely in treating positive law as an *object* of its investigative research on the basis of its rational and moral content. But positive law must never be mistaken for a *source* of knowledge. Just as it is not the job of medicine to research sickness merely as a phenomenon and to accept it as such, but rather to set *health* in opposition to it in order to overcome sickness, so the task of jurisprudence is to scrutinize positive law with regard to *its* health or sickness (i.e., with regard to its justice or injustice) in order to overcome injustice wherever it may be in force. Jurisprudence can only accomplish this task, however, if, instead of drowning so to speak in the phenomenology of the law that happens to be in force, it contemplates positive legal material from a *higher* vantage-point, whence it can judge and reconfigure that material.

There is no such higher vantage-point, however, *within* the field of positive law itself. This vantage-point can be found only if natural law and divine law, the two higher stages of legal consciousness, are present. Positive law can be *judged* only with a view to the ideal of law and to the rational and moral elements of the idea of law. If consciousness of the higher stages of law is lacking, there is no possibility of comparing what is with what ought to be. Uncritical acceptance of whatever law happens to be in force at a given time would signal the extinction of both natural and divine law from our consciousness, which would in turn signal the degeneration of the whole life of law into utilitarianism and sheer power. In short, such uncritical acceptance would mean the end both of jurisprudence and of the very consciousness of law.

Even were only one of the three stages of a complete knowledge of law lacking or separated off, this would mean not only that the knowledge of law is incomplete, but that it has also withered away.

If the consciousness of law does not experience law as an *ideal,* and as the highest value, it will lack the ability to orient itself, as well as moral seriousness and depth.

If the consciousness of law has also given up the *idea* of law, it will lose its connection with human culture in general and with its progress in history. It will drop out of the spiritual current of world history and become merely particular, provincial, and eclectic (e.g., national).

30

Going a step further, if the consciousness of law were to lose even the *concept* of law, there would no longer exist any consciousness whatsoever of law, but only a consciousness of power and ambition.

⊕

Lamentably, this path of the loss of the higher stages of legal consciousness is the one trodden by the prevailing current within jurisprudence in our day. The original unity of divine law, natural law, and positive law has been lost. Consciousness of divine law (the *ideal*) was first obscured; then consciousness of natural law (the *idea*) was pushed into the background; and finally, even positive law (the *concept*) was replaced by the concept of power.

Thus there emerged a tendency lacking ideal or idea. Nothing remained therein but a falsified concept of law. This is *positivism* pure and simple, whose practical effects in the dictatorships and one-party states of the present day have shown themselves clearly enough, and which have cost humanity enough blood and tears already. This tendency is the outcome of a gradual blinding of the consciousness of law, a process that took place in parallel with an overall going-blind to moral and spiritual values. It began with the divine law fell prey to the darkness of neglect, yielding its ruling position to "humanistic" natural law, which in turn had to beat a retreat before the "rational-subjectivist" natural law that characterized the Enlightenment and the French Revolution, with their absolutism of emancipated human reason. And finally, this rational-subjectivist natural law was pushed into the background by *pure positivism*.[11] As matters

---

[11] Even if one confines oneself to international law, the rise of pure positivism was already underway in the 1870s, and the compromise posi-

stand now, this pure positivism holds sway as the final stage of the degeneration of legal consciousness.

⊕

But this need not remain the final stage. A further stage of degeneration may yet be possible. We need only call to mind that, since pure positivism refers to the *wills* of the current power-holders as the sole source of the law in force, we human beings might also concern ourselves with the forces and influences that in turn determine those very wills themselves. Were this to happen, we would have arrived at the level of the *biological drives* at work in the human unconscious—those drives, that is, which we share in common with the lower orders of nature. These drives, for example the drive to self-preservation or "will to power" (the drive to devour the weak or press them into our own service) could then be declared the "primal source" of law. In the end, we could even go so far as to regard the *electromagnetic currents* produced by the material processes of the human organism as the source and criterion of the legal order.

The catastrophic debacle of the last decades, however, bids every honest and responsibly thinking human being to

---

tion of the "Grotius school" (e.g., Klüber, Martens, Wheaten, W. Scott, Heffter, Phillimore, Halleck, Bluntschli, etc.) had to retreat in the face of this. A series of purely positivistic treatises begins with Hartmann's *Institutionen des praktischen Völkerrechts in Friedenszeiten* [Institutes of Practical International Law in Peacetime]; for example, Hall (1880), Holtzendorff (1885), Wharton (1886), Bulmering (1887), Lawrence and Walker (1895), Rivier (1896), Lizst (1898), Ullmann (1898), then Oppenheim, Hannis, Taylor, Wilson, Maxey, Westlake, Méringhac, Diena, Hershey, Stockton, and others. See Oppenheim, *International Law*, vol. I, section 59 (4th edition, London, 1928).

come to a *halt* along this path. For this, we need only remind ourselves that there are *two* ways one can arrive at insight into the correct and the incorrect: along the path of immediate insight into the truth-content of what is correct, or along the path of the *reductio ad absurdum* by means of catastrophes. If, for a time, the consciousness of law gave up its insight into the truth-content of its two higher stages, and came to believe it could get along without them, it has need now to learn, along the path of catastrophe, that it has been going the wrong way. Indeed, jurisprudence is there precisely to help spare humanity catastrophes by knowing how to bring about, along the path of insight, what is right *before* catastrophe hits. Sadly, however, there is no reason to assume that the 1939–1945 war has attained the *final* stage of horror, devastation, and cruelty. On the contrary, the next war will *begin* with the tools that were deployed at the *end* of that one. A cloud of flying bombs will suddenly rain down upon a country's cities from a great distance. Such will be the beginning of the next war, if in the meantime a legal order for the whole of humanity is not established, an order in which divine law and natural law come to be honored once again as a right or law of humankind. What, then, is the content of a law that, instead of withering or becoming obscured, is a *complete* law as a reality in the world, in culture, and in the consciousness of the individual?

⊕

The *complete* conception of law rests in the first place on the insight that the world is an ordered whole, in the second place that the world order is of a moral kind, and in the third place that humankind as a whole is called to order its own life in such a way (through the application of its creative capacities) that it stands in accord with the moral world order. *Episteme*, as a capacity for immediate insight into the moral world order, underpins the consciousness of law and injustice. Thus, only a subordination of personal will[12] that has taken place out of free conviction can be described as, and established as, law. It is the authority of the moral force that orders the world—that is, the authority of God lends to law *moral authority* over personal will.

It was the truth and saving power of the primordial law, which embraced religion, ethics, and law, that led human beings to place that primordial law *above* their personal wills. Moreover, the catastrophic consequences of *not* subordinating the subjective will to law strengthened the conviction of the saving power of law, and compelled human beings to obey it. The essential core that first really "made law into law" (i.e., endowed it with inner authority) is the fact that it came into being out of caring *goodwill*, which it also mandates. Whether one looks at the *Laws of Manu*, at those of the *Zend Avesta*, or at those of the *Pentateuch*, it is always a question of the spiritual and physical well-being of people and of educating them in reciprocal goodwill. This goodwill blossoms, however, most completely and intensely in *Christianity*, which comes, not to destroy, but to fulfill the law[13] (that is, to reveal its true nature as an ideal). Here is revealed the complete and pure ideal of law as the combined obligatoriness of religion, ethics, custom, and law. The commands of *love* represent the result of the highest

[12] *Willkür*: "will" in the sense of being arbitrary, merely personal, or subjective. ED

[13] "Do not think that I have come to abolish the law or the prophets; I have come not to abolish but to fulfill" (Matthew 5:17).

insight, the essence of the moral world order. The commands of love are the *ideal*. They are the true and only goal of all law.

A social order, an organization of humanity, and a culture that has most fully realized the ideal of love towards the highest value (i.e., towards God) and among people (i.e., towards our neighbor), is more *perfect* than other social orders, organizations, and cultures. One may regard Christianity as one will, but no objective or responsibly thinking person can deny that solidarity among people is to be preferred to their fragmentation; that the stronger serving the weaker is to be preferred to the exploitation of the weak by force; that respect and guardianship for spiritual and cultural values stands higher, culturally, than plebeian and revolutionary iconoclasm;[14] in brief, that what makes this life worthy of human beings are all the varied expressions of love in social and private life. Love, which is presented in Christianity as the ideal to all peoples and races of the world, is the absolute ideal: it is the *divine law* of all life under the law. Love alone signifies law's final foundation and justification, its developmental direction, and its goal. *Any* other ideal—by which we mean any other ideal sought or striven after in a different direction—can only lead to catastrophes, misfortune, sickness, and the death of cultures. This ideal of love, this absolute ideal, is the idea of law raised to the highest power. It is the idea that prevails in human consciousness as a natural structure, and in the creations of culture as the revelation that those creations bring.

---

[14] Both in the literal sense and in the figurative sense—which is sought, for example, even by the scientific "enlightenment."

If *love* is the ideal of law that stands *above* legal consciousness as its guiding star, then *justice* is the motivating force, the formative principle, of law—that is, the *idea* of law—at work in the consciousness of law so as to shape that consciousness. And just as the ideal of love represents the essential content of the third stage of law (i.e., the commands of *divine* law), so the idea of justice, as the essential content of the second stage of law, represents the content of *natural law*. The *striving* consciousness raises itself to the intuition and appreciation of divine law as an ideal; but even "just" a *healthy* consciousness may find within itself (as something naturally given) sufficient force of conscience and reason to grasp natural law as a postulate of justice. Just as steam becomes liquid water by means of cooling, and just as, by further cooling, water becomes solid ice, so by means of the "cooling" of its religious and moral content, the *ideal* of love becomes the *idea* of law, and by means of a further "cooling" (i.e., intellectualization) of its moral content, the idea of law becomes the *concept* of law.

If, in accordance with its deepest nature (i.e., as an *ideal*), law is the intuition (*episteme*) of the moral world order, then its *effect* in the ordering of the human community consists in the sense of justice that forms the content of the *idea* of law. That this content will always be moral goes without saying, since its inner nature, the *ideal* in which this idea is rooted, is religious. Either one is thinking of absolutely no content at all when one utters the words "idea of law," or one is thinking of a moral content: which is no other than the justice that orders human society.

In the living practice of law, for example in legislation, it is, however, a matter only of the degree of justice that is *reasonable for all*. This degree of justice is the content of the *concept* of law that can be acquired from the *appearances* of positive law. For every positive law must not only be either useful for or necessary to the common good and not conflict with any higher obligations, but must also be physically and morally *possible*. A law is only morally possible, however, when the demands it places upon the current state of development of those to whom it is addressed do not exceed what is possible for them. This is what is meant by stipulating that those demands must be *reasonable*. From this it follows that the measure of "what is reasonable" can be variously limited among different peoples and in different ages according to the general level of culture they have attained. The measure of what is reasonable is a *relative* quantity contingent upon the cultural relationships prevailing at any given place and time. For the *present* time, and for the cultural situation of *European Christian humanity*, the content of the concept of law (as the degree of justice that is reasonable for all of Christian humanity today) can be sketched roughly as follows:

> Law is freedom limited by equality and by the obligations that other universally recognized values bring with them.

This formulation holds in equilibrium the *freedom* of the person (as the basis of private law) and the person's *obligations* towards higher values (as the basis of public law). For although I have the *right*, for example, to dispose of my own property as I see fit, this right may not impair the freedom of other persons (i.e., the others have the right to the same freedom as I have) and may not infringe upon those *obligations* that higher values (e.g., cultural assets, the international legal community, the state) bring with them.

Private law governs the *relationship* of people with each other as free persons; it represents the "horizontal" dimension of being *alongside* one another. Public law, by contrast, brings into force the principle of *subordination*, the "vertical" dimension of being *above or below* one another, and accordingly it brings with it a scale of values. Thus the content of the modern concept of law results in something like the figure of a cross, in which the vertical represents the *obligating* element in public law, and the horizontal the *justifying* element in private law.

Since we are concerned here only with a brief exposition of the legal-philosophical *principles* presupposed in any study devoted to *international law* as its particular subject, we will have to omit other considerations that could have been further developed here (in a number of possible directions) concerning the problems discussed above. For the purpose of an introductory consensus regarding the basic concepts that are to be presupposed, let it suffice that we summarize the results of the above observations in the following way:

(1) The complete form of law embraces three stages: divine law, natural law, and positive law.

(2) The essential core of divine law is the *ideal* of all law; the essence of natural law is the *idea* of law; positive law has the *concept* of law at its center.

(3) The content of the ideal of law is *love*, as it was revealed to humankind by Christianity. The content of the idea of law is *justice*, as it is at work in the human capacity for reason and conscience. The content of the concept of law is the *degree* of *justice* that is currently reasonable, i.e., the currently possible and necessary

quantity of tension and equilibrium between *justice* and *obligation* in a free person.

V. The Concept, Idea, and Ideal of International Law as a Law of Humankind

If we are in possession of an "adequate" concept of law, of a comprehensive idea of law, and of the highest ideal of law, then we need only apply these consistently and correctly in order then to comprehend the nature of *international law* as a concept, to understand it as an idea, and to know it as an ideal. For the whole life of law is by its very nature a *unity*. There are not two kinds of law that are different by nature, one inside and the other outside the state. Just as there is only *one* logic, so that the principle "the part is smaller than the whole" holds true both at home and abroad also, so "law is law" both at home and abroad. Its *application* may differ, but in its nature it is immutable—if it really *is* law. There are assuredly many degrees of lawlessness and injustice in our world, but where law *itself* is concerned, it is always the same law—it can only differ in *degree*.

This point is self-evidently true of European Christian humanity, but is not limited to this context. Even the most savage tribes have an awareness of law, and the law in force among them is a degree of the same one law. If there is a rule in force among a tribe of cannibals that one should devour those of one's enemies who have fallen in battle or whom one has taken prisoner, the substantive meaning of this rule is that one may *not* devour members of one's own tribe or those who belong to friendly tribes. It is a question, not of permission being granted to eat people, but of the *restriction* of this practice to "enemies" (i.e., to those beings who, according to this limited consciousness, do not really count as *people*). That their conception of humankind and of humane behavior is so restricted need not be grounds to call for any particular deprecation of the worth of these tribes. To see this, we need only recall that this same conception was championed as the ruling doctrine and practice in Germany under the National Socialists. There, too, "non-Aryans" were held not to be human, and so enjoyed no right to property, freedom, or life. During the war years, the same was true as well of "non-proletarians" in Soviet Russia: those who belonged to the bourgeois and noble classes were similarly refused the right to property, freedom, or life.

The fact that in certain European states of the twentieth century the conception of humanity was in all essentials on a par with that of cannibal tribes shows that, sooner or later, deviation from Christianity as the ideal of law *must* necessarily lead to "absolute cannibalism." For if we jettison the idea of the brotherhood of humanity as applicable to all races, peoples, and classes, we *ipso facto* restrict the idea of humanity to *one* race, *one* people, or *one* class. In short, we confess ourselves to have essentially the same conception of humanity as that which underlies tribal cannibalism. This conception of humanity, however, brings with it a very low stage of law, a stage that is as low as its conception of humankind is limited.

The *Concept* of International Law: *Family of Humankind*

Now, international law, which by right ought not to be tribal law, national law, or class law, but the right or law of humankind [*jus humanitatis*], is not conceivable if the idea of the fraternal unity and equality in value of all humankind as a matter of principle is lacking. Just as private law is not conceivable without the concept of *free personhood*, so international law as a right of humankind is not conceivable without the concept of the *family of humankind* as the totality of all human persons inhabiting the earth—all of whom have equal claims upon the law and are of equal value.

We are not speaking merely of the biological relatedness of all human beings (which is obvious enough) but, as a matter of principle, of their equal value. It is certainly conceivable that we could recognize and emphasize the biological relatedness while at the same time (or even for this very reason!) valuing each individual person equally little, rather than equally highly. We need only recall the valuelessness of human beings in China, where (despite the very developed consciousness of the mutual relatedness of all the Chinese in the mind of that nation) dying and being born have come to be devalued to the point where they are now almost unremarked everyday occurrences. This circumstance is usually explained by reference to the country's overpopulation— i.e., just as the overproduction of goods lowers their price, so the "overproduction" of people lessens their value.

We should take note, however, that both the fact of this devaluation and its "explanation" are rooted entirely in biology. This is a striking example of the truth that human *value* does not originate in the biological but in the *moral* realm. Now, *biological* relatedness (which, again, is obvious enough) cannot give rise to the idea of equal worth or value that is necessary to any right of humankind that can be taken seriously—for this, *moral* and *spiritual* relatedness is necessary. If the absolute value of an individual person as a *soul* is recognized, the same (absolute) value of the human *community* can also be recognized; and thus, too, both the equal *rights* of all human beings to property, freedom, and life, and the equal *duties* of all human beings not only to respect the property, freedom, and life of others, but to protect and further these values, and still higher values.

A humanity consisting of *biological* unities of relatedness can have neither rights nor duties—it can only follow its *needs* and retreat before the compulsion of the greater *power*. A community of human beings consisting of *souls*, by contrast, is the bearer of freedom, and therefore *is* capable of rights and duties. Just as law as such is inconceivable without free *personhood* (i.e., without a soul, which is the core of the being), any international law worthy of being taken seriously is inconceivable without the idea of the *relatedness of souls*—that is, without the absolutely equal value and fraternal belonging-together of all human beings.

The *Idea* of International Law: *Peace*

The *idea* lying at the basis of international law as its *sine qua non* is that of *humankind* as the *community of free beings* related to each other in soul and body. This idea stands in fundamental opposition to any fragmentation (i.e., division by opposition) of humanity into tribes, peoples, races, states, classes, and so on. For its essential manifestation or revelation is *peace*. Peace, not merely in the sense of absence of military action, but also in that of absence of *conflict* as such in all areas of life. Peace is the opposite of the struggle for existence that rules sub-human nature. Peace places the idea of *humankind*, as a fundamental law of the development of the human, in opposition to the idea of *bestiality* (the struggle for existence as the fundamental law of the development of the animal). War, class struggle, and economic competition are expressions of human nature that, in terms of their *negative* significance, the idea of human

justice is meant to set right and redress. The *positive* significance of the idea of human justice, on the other hand, consists in the *realization* of justice (i.e., of a humane legal
order) in the sense that all human beings are equally free
and equally obligated.

Even so, the realization of justice is not an end in itself. It
is merely the creation of an *order* that includes the requisite
conditions for the development of what is human as such,
in opposition to what is bestial. At stake is the development
of what is human. This is the real goal served by the order
of justice. For if the idea of international law as a right of
humankind has for its content the equal value of all the free
persons of which humankind is composed, it is not solely a
matter of recognizing the *current* stage of the development
of the value of what is human, but of *bringing that development of value to completion.* This is what is meant by the
ideal of international law as a right of humankind, just as
justice is the *idea* of international law as a right of humankind.

The *Ideal* of International Law: *Humanness*

The *ideal* of international law as a right of humankind is
not so much concerned with removing *conflict,* understood
as an appearance of the bestial within the human legal
order (i.e., *overcoming* bestiality) as it is with *fostering* the
development of "humanness."[15] In terms of justice, the
human legal order represents the milieu in which *true
humanness* can develop. Humanness is what is, so to say,
contained in the "vessel" of the human legal order.

---

[15] *Humanität.* This could as well be rendered as "humaneness" or
even "humanity" (not in the sense of the collectivity of human beings,
but in that of the essence or quality of being human). ED

43

What is the content of this ideal? The bestial law of conflict is opposed by the human law of *peace*. But if peace were taken to mean nothing more than *absence* of conflict between states, races, peoples, and classes, it would actually be a state of *calm*[16]—although not the sort of calm that can give rise to creative activity. Peace only receives the latter meaning when the overcoming of what is bestial is not solely the "negative" of absence of conflict, but is instead the "positive" of a further development of what is human. In other words, it is not enough that peace should reign. *Use* must be made of that peace in a manner most worthy of human dignity. And this occurs when humankind develops its *creative* capacities rather than its destructive ones, and in particular when the capacity for *love*, which has so far been only scantily developed, is activated.

True humanness *is* creativity. But creativity presupposes love. Just as we cannot create a piece of music out of hatred, scorn, or indifference towards music, but only out of the love of music, so in all areas of life (if we exclude caricature or the theft of others' creations for the sake of their possession or destruction) we can create only out of the capacity for love. This experienced truth of life has always been known. Indeed, it is from this truth that we ascend to the intuition that the *world* was created out of love rather than out of indifference or hatred towards it. Materialism tries to paint a colossal picture of the creation of a world originating in indifference. But any who have themselves had the experience of what it *is* to create, and of how creation is *accomplished*, know well that the world can have only origi-

---

[16] *Ruhe*, with its further connotations also of quiet, rest, tranquility, silence, serenity, repose, composure, etc. ED

nated *in love*. For indifference is uncreative passivity, and hatred is destructive activity. Thus did we gain the conception of the *source* of all the creativity in the world, of the creator of the world, of God.

⊕

The full development of true humanity thus also means creative cooperation with God, active unification of human willing, feeling, and thinking with God's willing, feeling, and thinking of the world. Now, God's consciousness of the world is creative—that is, it works out of *love*. Since this is so, the task of humankind is also to develop love. This means that only what is brought into being out of love is truly human; and further, that only a human world-order established on the ground of love, preserved through love, and so formed as to foster love, is *truly* human.

The *ideal* and the *idea* of international law as a right or law of humankind can be expressed through the words of the angel's Christmas message so well known to all Christian people from childhood onwards:

> "Glory to God in the highest": this is the simplest and most comprehensive formula for the *ideal* of the unity of humankind.

> "Peace on earth": this is the formula for the *idea* of a human order.

> "Good will toward men": this is the formula for human positive law, i.e., the content of the true *concept* of international law as a right of humankind.

As regards the latter, positive law has the human will as its law-creating source—and more particularly a will directed

45

towards the idea and the ideal, i.e., a *good* will. We could say that contemporary international law, in all its statutes (i.e., the mutable *concept* of international law as a right of the humankind current today), has just so much of the content of a right of humankind as is to be expected from good will on the part of all people (according to the current state of development of their consciousness) towards the content of the idea of justice and the ideal of love.

⊕

The individual issues connected with these foundational considerations, which have only been outlined here, will be more fully developed below. In this introductory part of the study, we have only set in place the most important signposts, in order to indicate the path we must travel in further unfolding the foundations of international law as a right of humankind. These signposts are the same today as they were nineteen hundred years ago, and I am pleased to disclaim any originality, as regards either their content or the way in which they are formulated, by invoking the words of the angel's Christmas message as the expression of the *absolute foundation* of international law as a right of humankind. I am also mindful how very absurd those holy words must seem in the year 1945, juxtaposed as they are to the terrible experiences of the two world wars and the other revolutions that have followed. Nor do I have any illusions that my invocation of this Christmas message will escape being called "unscholarly"—given that only what displays as little as possible of the spirit and the form of the past counts as "scholarly" these days. Nevertheless, I have reason to feel confident that my reference to the old words is both justified and scholarly, because these words contain the *truth.* I have been taught this by the whole world of ideas with which I am concerned in connection with international law as a right of humankind, as well as by the bitter experience of the catastrophes through which I have lived, and through which I continue to live. I shall permit myself, then, to set out in the following formulas the *absolute* foundations of international law in its three stages as divine law, natural law, and positive law.

> *Glory to God in the highest,*
> *and on earth peace,*
> *good will toward men.*

2

The *Subject* of International Law as a Right of Humankind

I. International Law as a *Phenomenon*

ow that we have introduced the preconditions of international law as a right or law of humankind, as well as its *nature* as ideal, idea, and concept (i.e., both what it is and what it ought to be), we must consider international law as it has come to be *historically*, and as it stands before us today as a *phenomenon*. To start with, it presents itself in a fourfold manner:

(1) As the sum-total of the *rules* governing the legal interactions of the various politically organized groups of people, as these are actually *practiced*: first in the interaction of the originally Christian parts of the politically organized family of humanity, then as they have been tacitly adopted by the remainder of politically organized humanity.

(2) As the sum-total of valid *treaties* that those politically organized groups of people have contracted among themselves.

(3) As the *world-organization* of the community of international law—that is, as the sum-total of arrangements (institutions) commissioned and authorized to

bring into effect the rules and treaties mentioned in
(1) and (2).[1]

(4) As the present *written record* of the international
legal branch of jurisprudence, as well as all the arrangements, institutions, organizations, and individuals
who or which maintain this branch of jurisprudence in
connection with law, politics, the economy, and culture.

As present phenomena, these four constituents of international law can be described more briefly as (1) international
common law, (2) international treaties, (3) world-organization, and (4) jurisprudence of international law. To these we
now turn consecutively:

International common law includes the five domains listed
below:

- Certain clauses in diplomatic law: protected status
  of diplomats, their immunity from domestic legal
  compulsion, the extraterritoriality of diplomatic
  embassies, diplomats' freedom from direct and personal taxation, and their freedom of communication
  with the states they represent.

- The inviolability and independence of states.

---

[1] Cf. Pitman B. Potter, *An Introduction to the Study of International
Organisation* (London: Bell, 1929), 5. "Rules of law, however, are of scant
effect if unsupported by organs of government. It is here that international organization proper comes into view. The system of institutions
and practices of the creation and administration of these rules of international law, which govern the body of international intercourse, constitutes the existing international organization."

- The responsibilities under international law of states and other subjects of international law.
- The sacredness of treaties (*pacta sunt servanda*).[2]
- The right to take steps to defend oneself.

Treaties under international law are formal agreements reached by at least by two, and at most by all, subjects of international law (e.g., world postal treaties, statutes of the League of Nations, various peace treaties and trade agreements between states, concordats).

World-organization consists of the administrative organs of the legal community. To this belong the organs of diplomacy, of the League of Nations, of the courts of arbitration and supervision and enforcement of international agreements (e.g., the general assembly, the council, and the secretariat of the League of Nations, the court of arbitration in the Hague, the bureau of the world postal union in Bern, the international bureau of weights and measures in Paris, etc.).

Jurisprudence of international law belongs to the phenomenon of international law as the sum-total of the scholarly work (researching, checking, summarizing, creating) necessary for international law to be made. It thus belongs to international law as a phenomenon, just as the theory of strategy belongs to the phenomenon of waging war.

---

[2] Strupp, Kelsen, Verdross, and Anzillotti see in the proposition *pacta sunt servanda* the fundamental norm of all international law. "It is—this must be recognized and insisted upon—undoubtedly pre-juridical in its roots." Strupp, *Grundzüge des positiven Völkerrechts* [Basic Features of International Law] (Bonn, 1932), 11.

The *Subject* of a Right of Humankind

⊕

We have already asserted above that the *phenomenon* of international law confronts us at the outset as fourfold, as the totality of: (1) international common law, (2) treaties, (3) world-organization, and (4) jurisprudence of international law. In pursuing the subject in more detail, however, it is impossible to avoid colliding with the problem of the phenomenon of the *Church* as a public legal organization. This problem is raised by the Roman Catholic church in particular, since the Orthodox and Protestant churches have generally given over their sovereignty to the state, and so are represented as corporate bodies by their respective states. The Roman Catholic church, on the other hand, is not only a human organization, but represents itself also in international law. This latter property is in any case sufficient to confer upon the Holy See the rights of a subject of international law (which has also come about in practice). But the first property (the organization of the Catholic church as a body covering the entire world) raises the question of the relationship between this legal community and the legal community of humankind as a whole.

This question can be handled formally as well as substantively. If we undertake a formal treatment of the question, it must be admitted that as a part of public law, canon law (as it stands in the *codex canonici*) belongs in its entirety to the legal life and the legal order of humankind. On the other hand, if many authors conceive of and describe international law as "international public law," then canon law (which has at the same time a public legal nature, and is nearly the most "international" of all the domains of international law) belongs to the whole body of the valid statutes of international public law. Just as international economic life repre-

51

sents a particular domain of the international legal order, so also does the international organism of the Catholic church represent a domain of the international legal order.

The fact that *states*, as international legal subjects, are not competent in this domain, changes nothing as to how matters actually stand. At most, this fact shows that states are not the only authors of positive law. It must therefore be acknowledged formally:

> The Catholic church is a legal community ordered according to the definitions of the *codex iuris canonici*.
>
> Its law is a part of public law.
>
> Its valid law is a part of the international public law currently in force (i.e., part of public law as a right or law of humankind).

A substantive treatment of this question leads us to affirm that the Catholic church postulates, champions, guards, and strives to realize the two higher stages of a *complete* right or law of humankind—namely *divine* law as the "ideal" of all law, and *natural* law as the "idea" of a right or law of humankind. In addition to this, the Catholic church participates in the *positive* right or law of humankind in the form of *canon* law, which has international validity. It must be further affirmed, moreover, that the Catholic church represents an organization that is in principle *universally* human, and whose supreme leadership is *sovereign*. Consequently, it has a share not only in the principles of international law as a right of humankind, but also in the way international law is actually formed, both as law currently in force and as a world-organization.

So far as its nature and its aim are concerned, the Catholic church is of course not confined to the legal domain. It participates in principle in the *whole* culture of humanity. But precisely *because* it participates in the whole of human culture, it also shares in an especially important domain within that culture—namely the domain of international law as a right or law of humankind. And it shares in international law more particularly in its most fundamental part, in that it cares for divine law and natural law. It participates in the positive legal part of international law, on one hand through canon law, but on the other by taking up a position of independent judgment in relation to all legal phenomena of the human legal community—and by declaring to the hundreds of millions of people who belong to the Church that all legally valid obligations of states that contradict divine and natural law are non-binding and invalid. Finally, it participates in the world-organization, in that the Church itself represents such an organization—one that includes all races, peoples, and classes; and also, in that it brings about with all the means at its command the aim of international law: the establishment of world peace, in principle and in fact.

In my opinion, then, the Catholic church must be considered as belonging to international law as a *further* phenomenon (5) of the right or law of humankind, and in particular to *all* domains of international law, i.e., to (1) international common law, (2) the domain of treaties, (3) the domain of the world-organization, and (4) the domain of jurisprudence and legal scholarship (since the Church continually expresses its judgment of the way in which the law currently in force accords with or contradicts public law and natural law). Freemasonry, by contrast, cannot rightly claim participation in the phenomenon of international law conferred upon it, because according to the report of its own representatives, it is neither a world-organization with a central organ, nor (in its membership, work, and achievements) a *public* organization; but is, instead, of a *private*, if not secret, character. In the same way, the organizations and programmatic activity of the Marxist communist parties (for example the Third International) are not relevant here, because they are "international organizations" solely promoting the goals of a particular class, and thus lack a "human outlook"—that is, an outlook embracing all classes.

II. The *Sources* of International Law

What significance is to be ascribed to the five forms in which the domain of international law makes its appearance? Their significance is threefold: the *shaping* of international law preceding its being in force; its *being in force*; and finally, what comes after its being in force—namely, its *strengthening* and *enforcement*.

Recalling Montesquieu's doctrine of the threefold separation of powers, we could say that the meaning of the five fundamental phenomena of international law is legislative, judicial, and executive, where:

legislative means the process by which the statutes of international law come into being;

judicial means the legal validity of those statutes;

executive means all the measures and institutions created to ensure that the legally valid statutes are obeyed.

The change that these three terms have undergone from their original meanings in the context of natural law stems precisely from the difference between national law and international law. Whereas the nation-state has an organized standing legislature (e.g., in the form of a parliament), the international legal community relies on *persua-ding* its members to *agree*. For this reason, we can only speak here of an *analogous* application of national legal terminology to international law. Let us make a start, then, by discussing (rather than the legislative, judicial, and executive processes), the following instead:

- the process of the *formation* of the clauses of international law *preceding* their being in force;
- the *validity* of those clauses;
- and the *means by which those clauses are enforced.*

⊕

The phenomena of the domain of international law that have a *formative* significance and *precede* the validity of the clauses of international law, can be described as the *source* or spring of international law. Just as water must first rise to the surface to appear visibly as a spring, so must the clauses of international law first *come into being* before they can make their appearance in the domain of legal validity. At the spot where a clause of international law makes the transition from *not being* in force to *being* in force, its spring or source becomes evident *as a phenomenon*.

> When we see a stream of water and want to know whence it flows, we follow it upstream until we come to the spot where it rises naturally from the ground. On that spot, we say, is the source of the stream of water. We know very well that this source is not the cause of the existence of the stream of water. "Source" signifies only the natural rising of water from a certain spot of the ground, whatever natural causes there may

be for that rising. If we apply the conception of a water source in this sense to the term "source of law," the confusion as between source and cause cannot arise.[3]

This is the empirical standpoint that Oppenheim adopts for the concept "source of international law."

We wholly acknowledge that this standpoint is objective and well-grounded, but we must also emphasize its *incompleteness*. We are not only concerned with the *spot* where the water appears, but also with *how* the spring has *come into being*, and *how* its water is constituted. For this reason, we consider it necessary (since we are dealing here with *science* rather than merely with *practice*) to supplement the concept put forward by Oppenheim with *two* further stages: firstly, what he describes as the "cause" of international law, and secondly, the essential content that stands behind the cause (behind the *concept*) of the spring as its *idea* and *ideal*. Thus, when speaking in what follows about "sources of international law," we must understand by this not merely some known historical fact, but also the particular stream or current of thinking manifested in it; furthermore, we must *also* understand by this the spiritual and moral ideal that lies behind this current of thinking.

According to the prevailing doctrine,[4] the sources of positive international law are *common law* and *treaties*. Indeed, sometimes only a single source (that is, treaties) is recognized as such,[5] since even common law (customary law, *droit coutumier*) can be thought of as a series of "tacit treaties" con-

---

[3] Oppenheim, *International Law,* fourth edition (London, New York, and Toronto: Longmans, Green & Co., 1928), §15.

[4] E.g., Strupp, Oppenheim, Despagnet, and others.

[5] E.g., Liszt.

cluded by logical actions. Other sources are adduced in a supplementary way for *theoretical* international law (*droit des gens théorique*)—in particular, the written record of the juris-prudence of international law.

If we do not rest content with this partial conception of the sources of international law, however, but ask ourselves how we can arrive at a *total* understanding of the sources of international law as a right of humankind, we arrive at the following result:

(1) One of the five main forms of appearance, or phenom-ena, of international law, usually described as "common law" is (in its genuinely common-*law*[6] part) *natural law* that has come into force as a direct result of its rational and ethical content. It required no agreement, because it had already carried conviction by virtue of its content. It thus underpins conventional law, just as reason and morality as such first underpin the possibility that the law of treaties or contracts might come into being in the first place. For example, no treaty would be conceivable if the principle of fidelity and trust were not *already* recognized. The principle of *pacta sunt servanda*,[7] just like the principles of the inde-pendence and equal value of the parties to a treaty and of the inviolability of their representatives (envoys), make pos-sible the whole phenomenon of the world of treaties. These principles are the presuppositions lacking which the entire causal complex of the coming-into-being of a given treaty would not be conceivable. Without them, the process would be unintelligible.

---

[6] In contrast to the legally insignificant custom (*coutume et usage*, cus-tom, and usage).

[7] "Agreements must be kept."

(2) For its part, so-called "common law" (reasonableness and morality in international law that comes immediately into force) flows from the *same* source to which human culture owes its awareness of the *true* and the *good* as such—that is, from the domain of the *religious* worldview. The latter was once shared by all of Christendom, and the *after-effect* of this shared heritage is the very fact that the present international-legal human community exists at all. Nevertheless, only part of humanity (divided as it is into states, races, peoples, and classes) holds true to this shared worldview and continues to practice it around the world. By this we mean the Catholic church, which, as the only bearer and contemporary protectress of the tradition of Christendom, is still today the most universal champion of the Christian ideal.

From a *legal* point of view, then, the Catholic church is the most authoritative champion of the Christian worldview. For this reason, we may affirm that, even if some principles of natural law may happen to have been occasioned by one or another Christian denomination or sect, in the final analysis they all lead back indirectly (both as regards their content and their history) to the fundamental intuitions put forward in the past by the original and universal Christian church. The *ideals* of the religious unity of humankind are (and always were) upheld by the Catholic church. These are the ideals (which may also be shared by others) that are implicit in the orienting influence of reason and morality.

Of the five forms taken on by international law, then, the Catholic church, as traditional representative of the Christian worldview, has the role of championing the orienting spiritual effect on reason and morality that, for its part,

58

underpins the law of treaties. This influence of Christian *ideals* upon the *ideas* of natural law—ideas that go on to form the rational and moral basis of the law of treaties— has often enough proceeded *of itself* "naturally" in history. For this reason, the most important task of the *science* of *international law* is to ensure that this "natural" influence should instead proceed *consciously* and *unerringly*—with the *complete* and *consistent* development of all its consequences.

(3) The science of international law is, alongside its association with religion and the Church, a source of international law in particular insofar as its task is to consciously connect the realm of the ideal with the realm of empirical facts. Its proper domain is that of *reason*. Principles and their consequences are its most important concerns. The core of these concerns is the task of elevating the principles of reason so as to connect them with their guiding moral ideals, and conversely to follow these principles of reason as they subside into the practical reality of the law-in-force and of its instruments (for example, the world-organization), to test and shape them theoretically. Just as the proper task of the *Church* in the realm of international law is to identify the true ideals of international law, so the proper task of *jurisprudence* in this realm is to nurture the ideas of international law. In other words, the *stimuli* come from the ideals, whereas the *method* by means of which these ideals are to be rationally realized in actual empirical reality takes place through the actions of the subjects of international law, in that they *bring law into force* (e.g., by means of treaties). And this activity finds its final form in the construction of a *world-organization*.

(4) It follows from what has been said that the original source of all international law lies in the ideals of Christianity (these ideals being represented by the Catholic church in particular); that the next source is represented by a reasoning that is faithful to morality (represented by a jurisprudence aware of its task and faithful to that task); and that the one after that, the empirical "source" of international law is the clarification of the will of the members of the family of international law, which flows from legal argument and agreement (*consensus*). In sum, what has been *stimulated* by ideals, *caused* by ideas, and *developed* into the concepts represented by the law-in-force, is found, in the end, along the path of *consensus*—found, that is, when treaties are concluded and embodied finally in the totality of the institutions of international law, i.e., in the world-organization.

⊕

Treaties thus represent only the third step of the "ladder" of sources, the second step of which is natural law, and the first divine law. In other words, the *essence* of law is of divine origin. God is the *first* source of all law. Subsequently, law is recognized and elaborated through human reason. Reason is thus the *second* source of law, that is, law brought into force by the agreement of the declared wills of the people authorized to do so. Treaties, then, represent the *third* source of law in the domain of international law. This third source (treaties that have actually come into effect) evidently presupposes *persons* who contract a treaty, i.e., *subjects* of international law. And so now is the time to raise the question of the nature of the subjects of international law.

III. The State as *Subject* of International Law

The international law "in force" rests in the first place upon the way it is actually practiced, and on treaties. But by *whom* is it proper to bestow, whether by means of practice or by treaty, the property of "being in force" upon individual legal statutes? Who is concerned in the contracting of treaties binding in international law? Whose legally significant actions have the meaning of relevant international legal "practice"—i.e., the property of international "common law"? Who, in other words, is the *subject* of international law. In short, who is a *person* in international law?

Actual dealings in international law instruct us that it is the representative bodies of politically-organized groups of people settled in particular territories or *states* that contract treaties and perform actions in "common law." *States* therefore appear at first to be the subjects of international law. In actual international legal practice, however, the *pope* as head of the Catholic church also appears alongside the states in the capacity of a "person" in international law.

It is exclusively the *sovereign* state that appears as a subject fully capable of action, i.e., as fully capable of transacting business, committing offences, and being a party to treaties. But beyond this, there is a continual succession of subjects on a "sliding scale" who possess a limited capacity for participation within international law, whether of an active or of a passive kind: neutral states, insurgents, protectorates, mandated territories, the Knights of Malta, national minorities, and, in certain cases, even single individuals.

Let us first consider the subject that is completely capable of action under international law: the sovereign state. By "state" is universally understood the phenomenon of a

sovereign group of people represented by a government—
that is, a sovereign group of people politically organized
and settled within a certain territory. Thus, every inhabited
territory that is self-sufficiently organized politically and
independent of other equally self-sufficient politically-organized territories, counts as a state. This is the universal concept of a state. But *by what means* are the people of a state
shaped into a unity? What is the real basis of state-forma-
tion? What, in other words, is the *idea* that is manifested in
the phenomenon, and in the *concept*, of a state?

⊕

If a group of people organizes itself as a political community, this happens not only from motives of which the
founders of the new state are *conscious* but also for reasons
that can reach beyond those motives. For example, the
founders of Rome could not have been aware at the time of
founding what would become the Roman Empire; and yet
the *ideal*, the *factual* kernel, of the future world-empire was
already present in Rome's foundation. Thereafter, the *idea*
of the Roman Empire develops gradually over the centuries.
It was this idea that bestowed upon Roman politics its
astonishing consistency and continuity, just as it was
Roman *arms* that gave Rome its superiority. The Romans
were not physically larger, more numerous, or wealthier
than many other peoples of the Mediterranean cultures.
What allowed them to achieve a leading position was the
then unrivaled significance of the *idea* presiding over their
state as compared with the ideas presiding over other states.
Carthage, for example, was forced to retreat in the face of
Rome because it had nothing by way of a commercial spirit
that it could set against the idea of Roman law.

The *Subject* of a Right of Humankind

Ideas are the causes of the viability and historical significance of states. Indeed, it is ideas that make states into *subjects* of world history in the first place, whereas states that have come to lack ideas (by first relinquishing their significance and then denying their actual existence) become mere *objects* of world history. It is not merely economic utility, security concerns, or military prowess that hold together the various human elements belonging to the state, but, precisely, a particular *cultural value* of which there is a shared recognition, care, and guardianship.

Thus, the cultural value of the Holy Roman Empire, which represented opposition to the world of Islam and paganism, was Christianity. With the waning of Christian belief in the ruling upper strata of society and the rise of secular humanist endeavors, the Holy Roman Empire disintegrated into special interest groups. In place of its former all-embracing idea, limited conceptions (e.g., national self-determination) became more prominent and split Christendom into a number of political entities that moved ever more in the direction of the intellectually superficial principle of national self-determination. The consequence of deviation from the overarching Christian idea is *nationalism*. National Socialism and Fascism are only the most recent consequences of deviating from the ideals of religion towards the biologically misconceived basis of "blood and soil"—which is most decidedly not the reality that constitutes the essence of the state. That reality is made up of cultural values, which in turn come to be summarized in particular ideas.

Not so long ago historically, humanity experienced, in the founding of the United States, the emergence of a new state numbered among the leading world powers today. The emergence of this relatively new state is well-known and fully documented. Do we have here a case of "blood," of a "motherland" ruled on racial lines? Or of "soil" (recalling that the land had barely been occupied by three generations of colonists before it declared its independence)? Obviously not "blood," since the blood was mainly that of Englishmen at the time. Obviously not "soil," since it was the Native Americans who had cause to defend their "clod of earth" against the foreign intruders. And as for the American colonists themselves, they were still welcoming and encouraging a flood of "foreigners" a century after the Declaration of Independence!

The real reason for the emergence of the United States was neither national nor provincial. It lay in the consciousness of economic, political, religious, and personal *freedom*, as was given expression in the Declaration of Human Rights underpinning the American Constitution. "American democracy aims at a federal and democratic world-organization."[8] Or, as the American poet Walt Whitman rapturously sings in his poem *Ship of Democracy*:

> Sail—sail thy best, ship of Democracy!…
> Of value is thy freight, 'tis not the present only,
> The past is also stored in thee!
> Thou holdest not the venture of thyself alone—not of
>   the western continent alone;
> Earth's *résumé* entire floats on thy keel, O ship—is
> steadied by thy spars;
> With thee Time voyages in trust—the antecedent
> nations sink or swim with thee;

[8] Adolf Rein, *Die geschichtlichen Grundlagen des amerikanischen Lebens* (Königsberg, *Ausslandsstudien*, vol. 8).

With all their ancient struggles, martyrs, heroes, epics,
wars,
    thou bear'st the other continents;
Theirs, theirs as much as thine, the destination-port
    triumphant;
—Steer, steer with good strong band and wart eye,
    O helmsman—thou carryest great companions,
Venerable, priestly Asia sails this day with thee,
And royal, feudal Europe sails with thee.[9]

This *idea* ("earth's *résumé*") still endeavors to find its final realization in a world-organization beyond the political borders of the United States. This idea, which represents the *raison d'être* of the United States, provides a most essential contribution in the history of humankind.

What goes for the United States goes in principle for all states: they are "stages" and "kinds" of the realization of ideas. The variety of these ideas is the justification for the plurality of states. States exist alongside each other until such time as an idea embracing all individual ideas comes to be universally recognized. If that were to happen, individual states would quite naturally have to disappear, for their plurality is justified solely by the *relativity* of the varied ideas governing their existence. But this means (as historical experience unambiguously instructs us) that states have only a relative and temporary significance. That they exist at all is an expression of the fact that no *truly* human idea has yet come to prevail. The plurality of states is not an expression of the *perfection* of the stage of human culture at which we have thus far arrived, but of its *imperfection*.

[9] Several verses elided in the original edition have been restored, as further emphasizing the point being made. Ed

There is, then, no reason to value states as anything more than imperfect stages on the path to a *truly* human order. Thus there is all the more reason *not* to place them any higher than alongside (let alone above!) the Christian church. The modern idolatry of "statism" must be recognized for what it is. Surely, after the experiences of the Second World War, this ought not to be a difficult thing to recognize for anyone of sound mind!

⊕

Once the relative and temporary significance of states is recognized, it is natural to ask after the *idea* that embraces *all* its relative aspects as they come to expression historically in individual states. In other words, what is the idea of *the state as such*? Regarding this, Bluntschli says the following:

> If humanity is in truth a whole, if it is inspired by a common spirit, how can it not strive for the embodiment of its whole essence—i.e., seek to become a state? States limited by nationality have, on this account, only a relative truth and validity. The thinker cannot yet find in them the fulfillment of the highest idea of the state. To him, the state is a human organism, a human person. . . . The body of the state must therefore be modeled on the human body. The perfect state is therefore similar to humanity, visible in its body. The *world-state is the ideal of progressive humanity*. . . . The common consciousness of humanity is, admittedly, still imprisoned in a dream-like state, and is in many respects confused. . . . Only in later centuries will the realization of the world-state be seen. But the longing for such an organic life-community of all peoples has already become evident from time to time in

the previous history of the world, and civilized European humanity can already fix its gaze on the high goal. It is true that all historical attempts to realize the world-state have miscarried in the end. From this, however, the notion that such a goal is unattainable does not follow, any more than if the Christian church (which also carries within itself the hope of eventually embracing the whole of humanity) would conclude that it is an impossible goal only because it has thus far not been attained. Just as the Christian church cannot relinquish its faith that it is universal, so humane politics cannot relinquish its effort to organize the whole of humankind.[10]

These thoughts, expressed 70 [now, 145] years ago, not only have not lost anything of their significance, but on the contrary are more relevant than ever today. What Bluntschli then presented as a task for "later centuries" (i.e., as a distant ideal) has today—after the First World War, after the abandonment of the League of Nations, and after the Second World War—become the most important and pressing practical concern.[11] To organize the world legally and politically is at the present moment a task we can no longer *permit* ourselves to put off to later centuries if we hope to avoid enormous catastrophes. What Bluntschli saw as a substantive and essential necessity so many years ago is today forced upon us through our experience of catastrophe—that is, through a *reductio ad absurdum.*

[10] *Allgemeines Staatsrecht* I, 1.1., ch. 2 ("Weltstaat"), 1875–1876.
[11] Of course, the whole litany of conflicts, wars, and political machinations that have occurred since this book was first published, have only made this pressing concern the more urgent. ED

⊕

"The perfect state is therefore similar to humanity, visible in its body," says Bluntschli, therewith outlining the *idea* of the *state as such*. A world-organization modeled on "the human body" is the concrete realization of this idea. The *body*, however, is merely a form and a sum-total of organs of which consciousness, the *soul*, makes use. Consequently, we cannot assent without qualification to the proposition that "the world-state is the ideal of progressive humanity" because the *ideal* cannot consist in the "human organism" (or the bodily unity of humanity) being realized in the form of an organization. This is so, because the *bodily* unity of humanity must be preceded by the unity of its *soul*. The *ideal*, therefore, is no mere world-state. It is the state that expresses the moral and spiritual unity of *humankind*, the unity of the universal Christian *church* and the universal *state*: in which unity, the latter stands to the former as the body stands to the soul. The church may not *instate* itself[12] (that is, gradually become absorbed in the state); rather, the state must *christianize* and *universalize* itself (that is, *catholicize* itself, or make of itself an "ecclesia universalis")[13] until

---

[12] *Verstaatlichen.* Other possible translations would be "nationalize itself" or "politicize itself," but these are burdened with distracting connotations. Or else, "turn itself into a state," which would serve well enough, but at the cost of some symmetry in the presentation. ED

[13] *Verkirchlichen*, literally to "church" itself or "ecclesialize" itself; but as the verb is here coupled with "universalize," the translation "catholicize itself" seems more apt, as "catholic" means both "universal" (literally) and "pertaining to the Catholic church." Elsewhere, where the author expresses himself more eschatologically regarding the "universal church," the expression "ecclesia universalis" was introduced in translation, as also offered here. See *Lazarus: The Miracle of Resurrection in World History* (Brooklyn, NY: Angelico Press, 2022), i (note 1); 224 (note 6, cont'd). ED

it has realized its true ideal, that of the concord of "humane politics" with the divine commands of love.

The ideal of the state thus amounts to a *metamorphosis into a higher stage of existence*. It is the transformation of the human order of *justice* (the world-organization in the sense of natural law) into the human and divine order of *love* (the Christian world-organism in the sense of divine law). In other word, the *idea* of the state (the justly-organized unity of humankind) is the realization of natural law, whereas the *ideal* of the state is the realization in *human history* of *divine humanity* as the complete unity of two natures that at present still appear separated as the "secular state" and the "church."

The state is thus threefold. In the first place, it is a territory inhabited by a politically-organized group of people that is sovereign (i.e., independent of other similarly organized groups of people). In the second place (as long as the plurality of states itself continues), the state is an aspect of the idea of an order of justice embracing all humankind, an order that is at the same time this idea itself. Or, put another way, the state that actually reveals the *nature* of the state is the world-state. In the third place, the nature of the state reveals a striving towards the realization of the ideal of *divine humanity* in human culture—that is, the merging of the human order of natural law with the ecclesiastical order of divine law.

⊕

So far we have only considered the *positive* side of the concept, idea, and ideal of the state. As a result of the misuse of human freedom, however, these could equally well be turned toward the *negative*. Instead of the ideal of a divinized humankind,[14] the ideal of a humanized divine (a humankind deifying or idolizing *itself*)[15] could be striven for, thus aiming, not at the ecclesialization or "churching" of the state (i.e., its christianization and universalization) but at the politicization of the church (i.e., its secularization and provincialization), so as to found a world-state upon the absolute tyranny of "emancipated" human reason and will, of arbitrary discretion and arbitrary choice. The world-state can mean an elevated level of well-being for humanity, but it can also mean a powerful concentration camp for spiritual culture—one of the lowest levels of well-being, to be sure!

Which of these two directions in the realization of the world-state is taken will depend on the actual *ideal* being striven for. The ideal of the world-state contains a guiding star, but it also contains the greatest of dangers, since in the end this world-state can only be either *Christian*: a brotherly-sisterly community of free people under God (*res publica sub deo*); or *anti-Christian*: a powerful machinery of coercive power relationships. This double tendency is powerfully present in all modern states. Every state today has more or less the tendency to become deified, to be worshipped as an idol, to claim for itself the right to demand from individuals sacrifices of property, freedom, and life, even in cases where it cannot be supposed that those individuals could morally condone the purposes for which they are being asked to make such sacrifices. In their actions, states as acting "persons" often stand at a much lower moral level than the majority of the individuals whom they repre-

[14] *Gottmenschtums.*
[15] *Menschengöttertums.*

70

sent. Ought individuals to sacrifice their own morally higher conceptions of justice and injustice, truth and lying, good and evil, for the sake of the many state actions that are of lesser moral value? The "logic" of most states answers this question with an unequivocal *yes*. We, however, must consider any and all demands of the state that contradict natural law (the law of reason and conscience) and divine law (the content of Christian revelation) not only to be null and void, but as obliging us to resist them.

The state does have justified claims to obedience and loyalty *within the limits* of what contradicts neither natural law nor divine law. But should its claims overstep these limits, it becomes our duty to resist them. To the extent that the state is morally neutral and Christian, it is to be affirmed. To the extent that it is immoral and anti-Christian, it is to be denied. This is the only possible practical consequence for humanity of the fact of the mixed nature and the relativity of the state. It is also the only possible way to guard against the growth of the anti-Christian world-state in a timely fashion, and to further the preparation of the Christian world-state.

The moral, substantively-legal, and cultural-historical assessment of states on both their brighter and their darker sides brings with it an evaluation of them as *relative*. This, in turn, raises the question whether states are the sole and unlimited subjects of international law; and, if they are not, what factors limit their legality as subjects. In other words, what factors have a formative meaning in international law *alongside* states, and even *despite* them?

IV. International Law as
Law of States and Law of *Humankind*

According to the prevailing doctrine, every sovereign state is in principle protected, precisely by its quality of sovereignty, from the interference (intervention) of other states in its internal affairs. Insofar as its internal affairs are concerned, every state is like a world unto itself, a world within whose borders it alone makes all determinations. If it observes its obligations under international law and does not overstep the limits of its authorization under international law, it is as absolutely autonomous as is a physical person in private law.

The state cannot be compared with a *physical* person, however, but only with the *legal* person of private law—that is, with a "corporation" that acts through the instruments representing it. From this it follows that the corresponding instrument representing the human community (the government) is only capable of acting under international law if it is itself regularly constituted and authorized for relevant actions under international law. We are faced, then, with the following question: Is the *government* of a dictatorship capable of action under international law? Is the *state* represented by a dictatorship obligated by that dictatorship—i.e., is that state *actually* represented by it?

If we adopt the position of the doctrine that has so far prevailed—that the *state* is absolutely sovereign, so that it is in principle no concern of other states whether it is justly governed or not—the answer to the above question must be that *any* government of a state that *actually* has its hands on *power* is capable of action under international law; and furthermore, that the state represented by this dictatorial government *can* be obligated by it, as long as it is tacitly or expressly *recognized* by the other states. Now, the fact of recognition itself, by its nature, means nothing other in effect than *taking up a position* on the part of one state towards the internal relations of another state.

This, in principle, is the *first* stage of intervention. When a state will not recognize another state, the former expresses a *judgment* on the latter, a judgment laden with sanction-like consequences—such as the refusal to interact with the non-recognized state under international law, along with all the consequences this refusal may entail.[16]

The *second* stage of intervention would be the exertion of *diplomatic pressure* in the form of interceding (e.g., with "friendly advice").[17]

The *third* stage of intervention would be the application of political and economic *sanctions*.

The *fourth* stage of intervention would be *actual* intervention in the form of exercising pressure by means of armed force (blockade, policing expedition, war of intervention).

⊕

Actual practice thus contradicts the theory of the absolute sovereignty of the state. It is only a matter, then, of deciding whether the theory is right, and so actual practice is what infringes upon the law; or whether the theory is faulty, and so in a legal sense practice is ahead of it. In the theory of the

[16] Thus, the United States refused to recognize the government of the Emperor Maximilian set up in Mexico in 1863. This non-recognition was a *negative* act of intervention—that is, a counter-intervention with respect to France in Mexico.

[17] This is how Japan, for example, delivered an ultimatum to Germany in 1914.

absolute and inviolable sovereignty of the state, one starts from the position that the state and its current government are in principle *one*, and that, for their part, the people of the state and its government are also in principle *one*. The *inseparability* of the three factors (state, government, and people) underpins the idea of the "state" as an absolutely sovereign person under international law. The three are accepted and treated as it were *en bloc*, on the *presupposition* that the professed intentions of a government are at the same time the professed intentions of the "state," as a person under international law.

In brief: the state is conceived of as a unity of will. But, however necessary this political unity of will (or the will of the state as capable of action *as such*) may be, it is nevertheless a legal fiction (in treaties, for example) that can be valid only given certain presuppositions. These presuppositions are summarized by the basic condition that the government representing the people does not merely express its own conviction, but *actually* expresses the conviction of the people whom it represents—the people of whose will it is the instrument.

Now, the fiction of a unified will of the state can only be valid in those cases in which the quantitative *and* qualitative majority of the people unquestionably stands behind the government—not just the simple quantitative majority of citizens, but also the qualitative majority, i.e., those citizens who carry and foster its culture. In every case where this condition is not satisfied, the presupposition of the will of the state cannot hold. In such cases, we can at most speak of a government's *de facto* capacity (in the sense of mere power) for actions of state, but not of the will of the state—for the latter presupposes the unity of the people's will and the will of the government in the actions of the state. States where this unity of the people's will and the will of the government is not present, or is in doubt, can either not be recognized as a matter of principle, or else recognition previously granted them must be removed. In other words, they cannot be considered as capable of conducting business in an international-legal sense.

Since non-recognition is the *first* stage of intervention, however, the door is thereby opened to the three further stages of intensifying non-recognition (i.e., intervention) of this state. How far one wishes to intensify the activity of non-recognition of the state in question depends on the circumstances, and in particular upon whether there are reasons not only to *protect* the security of *treaties*, but also to *intervene* in the interests of *humankind*, of defense against *aggression*, and of defense of the *cultural treasures* of humankind. In principle, however, intervention can be carried out against any non-recognized or legally non-recognizable state (e.g., a dictatorship). *This* sort of state is, thus, *not* sovereign in the sense of the impermissibility of interventions against it, for it has no "will of the state"—meaning that under international law it is not a *person*.

⊕

However, it is not only non-representative, undemocratic states that can display one of the four grounds indicated above for intervention in its affairs if it damages or threatens to damage the "will of the state" of the human community—these grounds being, again, breaking a treaty, offense against humanity, aggressive conduct, and destruction or endangerment of universal human cultural treasures. Indeed, a state can be as democratic as you like, and the will of the people and of government can be in full accord; but even so, that state can *still* commit offenses under international law, or oppress a minority within the state through the will of the majority in a manner that crudely offends against humanity, or take a dangerously aggressive military position, or threaten values of universal human culture (e.g., the sacredness of religion) with destruction and desecration.

If such an offense against international law as a right or law of humankind occurs (an offense, that is, against abiding by a treaty, against security, against humankind, or against higher human cultural goods) by means of an act of real and indubitably ascertainable will of the state (that is, of the unity of will of a people and its government), then every individual state in the rest of the human community, and the whole body of states, have not only the right, but the *duty*, to apply the appropriate level of compulsion to the offending state in question. The sovereignty of the individual states ceases to apply when the border of *law-breaking* is crossed. This is the point where the realm of the higher sovereignty of *humankind* begins—the realm that not merely permits, but morally, logically, and legally *demands* intervention against the offending state.

For the private person, the consequences of law-breaking (claims for damages, enforcement of compensation, punishment) represent compulsions of the private person's will. Now, the consequences of law-breaking under international law ought to be just as binding for the will of a state as they are for a private person. But only *states* can exert this compulsion (whether individually or collectively is not at first the essential point), and in doing so they cannot avoid facing a dilemma. Either international law exists, and consequently there must be legal protection that will be empowered to prevent offenses against the statutes of international law, as well as to ensure that those offenses are accompanied by binding consequences; or else international law does *not* exist, which means that every individual state will comport itself according to its own power and the power of its neighbors.

If international law exists, however, it must be protected. It then becomes the *duty* of the states to commit themselves to international law as a *right of humankind*. This self-evident idea (that third-party states are obligated, individually or collectively, to put their means of power in the service of international law) has unfortunately been obfuscated by the influence of the theory that third-party states are not authorized, and therefore *a fortiori* cannot be obligated, to intervene.[18] This theory has not only been overtaken by the practice of states, and by what the historical events between 1914 and 1945 have taught us; it is also substantively, in both moral and legal terms, *highly unsatisfactory*. From the ethical point of view, its moral content can be summed up in Cain's objection: "Am I my brother's keeper?"

As far as the critique of this theory from a legal point of view is concerned, let us, with Stowell, allow Mr. Root to speak:

We have been proceeding upon the underlying theory that obtains in the civil law, using that term in its

---

[18] See Strupp: "*Intervention*, that is, the interference in any concern (internal or external) of another state when supported by force or the threat of force, *is always contrary to international law*. It infringes upon the principle of the independence of states, and also, sometimes, upon that of the equality among states." *Grundzüge des positiven Staatsrechts* (Bonn, 1932), 98.

restricted sense, as distinct from the criminal law, that whether one nation breaks its contract with another nation is nobody's concern except the two nations', the two contracting parties. That generally has been the principle applied to all international law; so that if two nations have a controversy, it is an act of impertinence for another nation to interfere in it. We will never have any substantial improvement until we adopt the other theory, which is that a controversy of physical violence between any nations is the direct concern of all nations; that is to say, by the application of the principle of keeping the peace which we apply in criminal law in our own communities. It is a matter of concern to me that two men get into a fight in the street, not because I am particularly concerned with them, but because, unless the law safeguarding peace and order in the community is enforced and maintained, somebody will attack me, my wife, or my child.

We must shift from the theory of treating the relations between nations as something depending on the law of contracts (and which concerns only the contracting parties) to the view under which the relations between nations are regarded as involving the maintenance of order in the community of nations (which is the concern of every independent country). As soon as that view is accepted, nations will no longer be fearful of intervening, and there will be no resentment because they do intervene; and the establishment of institutions for the assertion of the natural right of nations will be natural and appropriate and universally accepted. I think that is the beginning of all consideration of the future—the adoption of the theory that any war is the concern of every nation.[19]

This intuition, however—like every truth—is acquired not only by means of the free persuasion of the intellect, but also by force, as a result of the catastrophic course of history. Truths that one does not wish to *see* will make themselves recognized through catastrophes. This is the case with the theory of the law of intervention and the duty to intervene. If the great powers had obeyed the duty we are discussing, and *had* interfered in Germany's internal affairs in 1933, or at the latest by 1935, many millions of people's lives would have been spared, and tens of thousands of localities would have been spared also. Or is it possible even *today* to find a legal authority who will speak up in favor of the standpoint of non-intervention, and who will say that political, humanitarian, and ethical considerations should remain separate from purely juridical considerations—and that, from a purely juridical point of view, intervention is "always contrary to international law"? Such a formalistic intransigence would not even be able to appeal to the imposing maxim of legal fanatics, *pereat mundus, fiat justitia* ("let the world perish, so long as justice may be done"), since *justitia, justice,* consists precisely in protecting the peaceful and benevolent part of humanity from the misfortune of murder and destruction. And if intervention in the internal and external affairs of a state is the right means to this end, then it is, precisely, both materially and formally, *just.*

[19] In *Transactions of the American Society of Law*, 1918. On this, Stowell remarks that "few of our lawyers have Mr. Root's clear understanding of this matter, and the obligation of intervention is, unfortunately, not so generally recognized or so effectively sanctioned as it should be."

The sovereignty of every state *ceases* at the border of infringement upon divine law, natural law, and the law of treaties; and at that border there comes into being not merely the right, but also the unavoidable duty, for the community of states, and also for each state, to intervene. What would have become of humanity today if the leading states had maintained their position of non-intervention beyond 1938? If the conflict between Germany and Czechoslovakia, and that between Germany and Poland, had been regarded as a "private" matter between these pairs of states? Germany would have swallowed up another country every few months, and at the very least, the population of the European continent would have been divided into two large groups: those who marched and shouted with Hitler, and those who, as slaves, performed drudgery for him (if, that is, they did not find themselves in concentration camps). The doctrine of absolute non-intervention has been refuted not only on rational grounds and by what we have learned from catastrophic events, but also by the *practice* of states in political history.

Indeed, the practice of states furnishes so many examples of intervention on the grounds given above[20] that there can be no talk of the universal validity of the principle of non-interference. Thus Article 61 of the Berlin Treaty of 1878 explicitly hands the great powers of the European continent the right to interfere in the internal affairs of Turkey with respect to the Armenian provinces. Subsequently, the great powers repeatedly intervened to support the Armenians on the basis of the provisions of this treaty. Moreover, the

[20] Violation of treaties, prevention of aggression, humanitarian considerations, and the protection of ideal values.

The *Subject* of a Right of Humankind

guarantee contained in the Paris peace treaty of 1846 also
contain a collective guarantee on the part of the contracting
powers, a guarantee that carries with it the right of these
powers to intervene. There is indeed no lack of examples of
reciprocal intervention on the part of Christian and other
civilized countries. Thus the intervention of Great Britain
in the peace negotiations following the Franco-Prussian
war of 1870–71 prevented the levying of the full amount of
reparations that Germany wished to demand from a
defeated France. This intervention created much bad blood
in Germany, but forced it to desist from any resumption of
the war against France, now that France had Great Britain
as an ally. Similarly, in 1875 the great powers collectively
intervened with energetic representations to Berlin when it
was believed that Germany was planning an attack on
France. In 1835, Great Britain intervened in Spain so as to
prevent the Carlists from shooting their prisoners of war. In
1863, Great Britain, France, and Austro-Hungary made representations to the Russian government on the matter of
the oppression of their Polish subjects. After more than
three years of the Cuban civil war, the United States intervened in 1898 on humanitarian grounds to bring to an end
the atrocities that were repeatedly and extensively committed by the Spanish military on the civilian non-combatant
population of Cuba. This intervention led, as is well
known, to the Spanish-American war. In 1900, the great
powers collectively undertook armed intervention in China
to protect the international legal principle of diplomatic
immunity, since, during the Boxer Rebellion, a series of
embassies had been attacked and the German and Japanese
envoys had been murdered in Peking. When the Sultan of
Morocco, Mulai Abdelhafid (1909) tortured to death his

defeated political opponents (El-Rogui and his supporters), there followed a collective written representation on behalf of the whole diplomatic corps in Tangier, in which the Sultan was called upon to relinquish the use of torture in Morocco—and in the future to obey "the laws of humanity." The United States protested to the German government on November 29, 1916, against the deportation of Belgian civilians.

The list of cases of intervention could be very considerably expanded if one were to think about the intervention of great powers in order to secure observance of a treaty (for example, in respect of foreign state debt), to combat slavery, to protect minorities, and so on. Here it is only a matter of showing from examples that the doctrine of non-intervention was *not* universally recognized in the *practice* of states even before the foundation of the League of Nations. Even in the realm of pure theory, the legality of intervention on humanitarian grounds was recognized by a series of authorities—by, for example, Grotius, Wheaton, Heiberg, Woolsey, Bluntschli, Westlake, Fauchille, Rougier, Mandelstam, Stowell, and others.

Since the foundation of the League of Nations, however, the right to intervene has not only been universally recognized in practice, but in particular cases has also been raised to a statutory duty. Even collective interventions (as for example in the sanctions against Italy in the Italo-Abyssinian war) were recognized and technically organized as a normal mode of proceeding. In the final analysis, the goal, the meaning, and the justification for the *existence* of the League of Nations lies precisely in the fact that it is warranted, obliged, and able to meddle in those affairs of sovereign states that as a matter of fact or of principle concern the cultural community of humankind. The whole machinery of the League of Nations is only there to set limits, when need be, to the sovereignty of individual states—and then solely in the name of a higher sovereignty of humankind.[21]

In fact, the Covenant of the League of Nations signifies a decided deviation from the dogma of non-intervention. The provisions of articles 11 and 16 of the Covenant are the precise *opposite* of this dogma:

> Any war or threat of war, whether immediately affecting any of the Members of the League or not, is hereby declared a matter of concern to the whole League, and the League shall take any action that may be deemed wise and effectual to safeguard the peace of nations (Article 11). Should any Member of the League resort to war in disregard of its covenants under Articles 12, 13, or 15, it shall *ipso facto* be deemed to have committed an act of war against all other Members of the League. . . . (Article 16)

The obligation to register treaties with the secretariat of the League in order to make them legally binding (Article 19) is

[21] The preamble to the Covenant of the League of Nations contains the assertion that the interests of humanity as a whole take precedence over the interests of individual states. It thus speaks of particular *obligations* of the individual states to respect the right of humankind, i.e., "to promote international cooperation and to achieve international peace and security." The principle of collective intervention not only underpins the whole Covenant of the League of Nations, but is also expressed within it. The members of the League avow the principle that the maintenance of peace demands *the reduction of national armaments to the lowest point consistent with national safety and the enforcement by common action of international obligations* (Article 8).

in itself a far-reaching step in the direction of limiting the sovereignty of states in the interests of everyone, and in fact represents a permanent institution of intervention in the affairs of the individual states contracting the treaty.

⊕

The objection that it is the states themselves that voluntarily lay these constraints upon themselves, and that in consequence the constraints are really only an expression of the sovereign wills of the individual states that happen to possess the property of *external* compulsion, misses the point that there is also an *inner* compulsion of the will by law, reason, and ethical life. This inner compulsion does not remain hidden in the realm of the subjective. It also makes its appearance in an objectively perceptible way—both in the forum of *public opinion* and in the *events of world history.*

The public opinion of *people* (who represent the actual reality of the state) can compel the "sovereign will of the state" to actions that can lead to the state's placing far-reaching limitations on its own will. Indeed, it can in principle lead even to the surrender of that sovereignty. Law, reason, and ethical life are, however, the forces that for their part determine public opinion insofar as it is healthy (i.e., insofar as it does not conflict with international law as a right of humankind).

Alongside the force of the reaction of individual, or of all, members of the international legal community (e.g., taking matters into one's own hands, intervention) to breaches of international law on the part of a state or group of states, and alongside the force of public opinion both within the state or states concerned and in the rest of the world, international law also possesses a third force apart from any organized apparatus of sanctions that provides perhaps the most effective sanction of all. This is the force of the "court of world-history."

Let us give room for the French jurist Frantz Despagnet to speak on this topic:

> Violence calls forth reprisals sooner or later; an abusive treaty imposed by force prepares for the revenge of a whole people in future, a people who may take a very long time to gather together the resources necessary to effect it. The brevity of human life does not always allow us to see the violation of international law and the consequences that afflict the violators; but if one observes the course of events as a whole over a long period of time, one is struck by the evident harmony between respect for international law and the prosperity of peoples, as against their misdeeds and their misfortunes.
>
> When M. Thiers asked Germany, after the fall of the Second Empire, "on whom are you waging war?" the famous German historian Ranke replied, with deep meaning, and evoking the memories of the Palatinate's being laid waste, "on Louis XIV!" "The history of the world" is indeed, in Schiller's sublime expression, "the world's judgment." In another way, history shows us in a striking manner the penalties for infringing the *ius gentium* (*droit des gens*). If, as Montesquieu showed, governments perish when they abuse their own principles, all foreign policy contrary to Law finds its punishment in its own excesses. France offers striking examples, particularly those of Louis XIV and Napoleon. It has even been said that there is no other

penalty in international law, but that this one is enough, since it is implacable and fatal.[22]

⊕

The three kinds of sanction of international law as a right of humankind (i.e., the organized protection of international law by the community of states, public opinion, and the court of world history) correspond to the three areas wherein cooperation of the concept, idea, and ideal of international law can appear as a whole. These are the areas of positive international law, of natural law, and of divine law. Each of these represents not only a further substantive stage of consciousness and of legal validity, but a different way of effecting sanctions. Whereas positive law brings along with it an organized protection of its statutes (in the form of taking matters into one's own hands and of the *intervention* of states, whether individual or collective), the sanction of natural law consists in the effect of *public opinion*, while offenses against divine law are punished and compensated for by the court of *world history.*

Divine law is sanctioned by what prevails in world history. The Book of Revelation, then, is the penal law code of the divine law of the nations before the judgment seat of world history, i.e., of divine justice. Public opinion, as an expression of the reason and conscience of humanity, represents the sanctioning power of natural law. Finally, treaties and alliances between states that are contracted to protect the international law in force are the means to lend weight to positive international law by means of force.

Thus, the apparently "supreme" sovereignty of the state is

---

[22] Cited in A. Sorel, *L'Europe et la Révolution*, i, 35.

limited (1) by the positive legal statutes of the community of states, (2) by the public opinion of the human cultural community, and (3) through the governance of world history by a higher power. State sovereignty must give way to three higher states of sovereignty: to the sole perfect and supreme sovereignty of *God*, which governs world history; to the sovereignty of *humankind*, which reveals itself as reason and conscience in public opinion; and to the sovereignty of *the law that is in force* in treaties and in practice among the community of states. As for sovereignty of the *state*, it only comes as a fourth sovereign authority, and consequently as a fourth source of authority, for *individual persons*.

⊕

Thus, the individual *person* stands, first of all, immediately under the sovereign authority of divine law. The first question the individual must ask when considering the legality of a course of conduct is whether this conduct is in accord with divine law. If it does not conflict with the commands and prohibitions of divine law, it must then be further considered whether it does or does not contradict human reason and custom; if it does not, it must be ascertained further whether it damages the interests of humankind in the given situation; and finally, it must be asked whether it is permitted by the laws of the state in which that individual resides. This is the true and humane order of the questions raised above. Millions of victims of the World War between 1939 and 1945 died to make possible *this* order of questions, since the Hitlerism against which they fought was in essence nothing other than asking the above questions in *reverse* order.

In Hitlerism and Fascism, the state is the highest authority. It is endowed with absolute sovereignty. God, humanity, reason, and conscience must all fall silent in face of it. Since it was precisely *this* view that was contested during the war, it must also now be contested after the war, wherever it so much as begins to make an appearance. Otherwise, the war will not have achieved its actual goal.

Now, the effective combatting of a false view consists in replacing it with the correct one, which in this case is the opposite of the false one. In other words, it is correct to place divine law above, reason in second place, international law in third place, and the positive law of one's own state in *last* place. Only this counts as true anti-Fascism.

The formula "my country right or wrong" is the maxim of the behavior (contrary to international law) that caused this world war, and that the world war was fought to defeat. After having defeated Hitler, Mussolini, and their Japanese imitators at the cost of such sacrifices, should we allow the dangerous ideology of Hitlerism to live on, and to bear fruit? For Hitlerism is the standpoint that idolizes the state, that places the state *above* the whole of humankind, above even the highest spiritual values. "Hitlerism" in this sense need not be restricted to Germany: the experiences of recent years have shown that in almost all countries there were, there are, and there will be "Quislings"[23] in the hundreds of thousands. These people need not belong to a common political party, but common to them all, right across the world, is the "inverted consciousness of law,"

---

[23] A collective name for people with an "inverted consciousness of law" such as Laval, Mussert, Tissa, Degrelle, etc., and, last but not least, Quisling himself. ED

which is the ideological, essential core of Hitlerism. Accordingly, any who place the sovereignty and authority of their own state above that of international law, natural law, and divine law—or who *a fortiori* deny the existence of these higher stages of law—are champions and continuators of Hitlerism in the world, of that ideology which *must* lead to conflict of *one* people and *one* state against all other peoples and states.

In face of this radical realization, we come to see—to our horror—that, this being the case, many great people in the past, and many influential personalities in the present, fall (according to this definition) under the rubric of "Hitlerism." How, we might well ask, would matters stand in this respect with Cardinal Richelieu? On this topic, we have to say that after the dreadful catastrophe of the last world war, there is hardly a single area in which it is not necessary that we *unlearn* everything and *re-learn* it.

⊕

Today there are many things that have to be unlearned and re-learned, not least world history itself. For Hitler did not come out of nowhere. His appearance and his success are the result of a long preparatory process in world history. He is the fruit of a tree that has been growing for centuries. Trees, however, are to be known by their fruit. When we have realized that the fruit brings disaster, we must have the cognitive courage to recognize that the tree which bore this fruit brings disaster also. If Hitler is a disastrous phenomenon, then his spiritual "family tree" (the tendency within culture that prepared for his coming, his effectiveness, and his success) is to be judged disastrous for humanity too. To Hitler's family tree belong, as his forerunners, all those politicians and leaders of the past who placed *raison d'état*[24] above humaneness, humanity, and religion. Richelieu, too, was decidedly one of these bringers of disaster to humanity—along with many politicians and ideologues of earlier and later centuries, among whom we might number not least Bismarck, the founder of the Prusso-centric German empire. The Holy Roman Empire of Charles V was founded with the intent of serving Christianity and Christendom. The "Unholy" German Empire, by contrast, was founded with the intent of developing and expanding itself at the expense of others by means of power. In Hitler, it attained its goal.

Well, this empire lies in ruins now, both literally and figuratively, that is, politically. Should we stand patiently by and wait to see where the *ideology* out of which this empire emerged will again build an empire for itself? Having hacked off the fruits and branches of the evil tree, should we leave its trunk and roots untouched?

But the root of this tree is the inverted consciousness of law, and its trunk is no other than the self-serving politics of *raison d'état*! We will not be safe from further assaults upon humanity until we have *once again* learned to direct thinking first of all to God, and only last to the concerns of states and their own power.

⊕

What we have described here as the "inverted consciousness of law" is only a partial manifestation of the far broader ten-

[24] "Reason of state": a purely political reason for governmental action, based on national interest and often violating principles of justice—usually associated with Cardinal Richelieu's "grand strategy" during the Thirty-Years War. ED

dency that is becoming visible in all areas of culture, the tendency to "inverted consciousness" *as such*. The primary distinguishing feature of this inverted consciousness is the so-called "revaluation of all values"—that is, conceiving of the lower as the higher and the higher as the lower. Friedrich Nietzsche was one of the most prominent champions of this inverted consciousness. His "super-man" developing his "will to power" "beyond good and evil" is in reality no super-man at all, but an "inverted-man" who, instead of assigning goals and duties to his will with his thinking-consciousness (as is the case with a "man-man"), has *subordinated* himself to the will, and is therefore no more than the will's executive instrument.[25]

The super-man of Nietzsche must, as a matter of course, stand *beyond* good and evil, for, having let fall the reins of reason and conscience in favor of the "will to power," he has lost his moral consciousness. What Nietzsche put forward in his writings as an ideal became in Hitler a reality. If from this point of view we read Hitler's book *Mein Kampf*, it becomes evident that Hitler was a person in whom the normal relationship between thinking and willing was inverted. For him, it is what he *wills* that counts as "true." The only task incumbent upon thinking is to *carry out* the particulars of executing the commands of the will. In other words, whereas *we* submit our will to the truth that shines into our thinking (the truth being for us something of higher rank than our wishes), for *Hitler* there is no truth in this sense.

---

[25] The author revisits this theme in chapter 8, "Christianity as Ongoing Resurrection of Divine-Human History (*Ecclesia universalis*)," in *Lazarus: The Miracle of Resurrection in World History* (Brooklyn, NY: Angelico Press, 2022), 211–18.

Hitler lacks any awareness of truth. Where we experience the truth, he experiences only the contents of his personal will. From the standpoint of truth and truthfulness as we experience them, such a constitution—in which thinking is only a tool whose purpose is to render the contents of one's personal will plausible to the world—is actually a consummate "propaganda apparatus." From the standpoint of force and coercion, such a constitution is a consummate "power apparatus" in the sense of the "will to power" of the Nietzschean "super-man."

This inversion of the relationship between truth and power, which we find in Nietzsche as an ideal, and in Hitler as a reality, is however not limited to these two people. It occurs in many others and in many fields. It is only that, in others, the inversion has not reached the full hundred and eighty degrees it did in Hitler, but has so far settled in at various degrees along the scale to full inversion. In some people it has reached forty-five degrees, in others as many as ninety, and so on. Whatever its degree may be, however, the process of inverting the relationship between truth and power is underway almost everywhere—and not least of all in the realm of *legal* life, where it appears in the form of the tendency to exclude law *in-itself* and to replace it with the *power* of the state, or of the states.

Pure positivism in the realm of legal life is an expression of the wider phenomenon of "inverted consciousness" as an inversion of the relationship between thinking and willing. Here, the same inversion occurs in the relationship between law and power. In this case, "law" stands for the intellectual experience of truth, and "power" for the development of the strength of the will. Our task, then (if we wish to bring *healthy* consciousness to prevail once again in the field of international law), is to restore a healthy relationship between law and power in *theory*, and where possible in *practice* too. This task will only have good prospects of success if the basic dogma of positivistically-oriented international law (i.e., the idea that international law is nothing but the *law of states*) can be replaced by the other view, namely, that international law is a *right of humankind*, oriented towards divine law and grounded in human reason, in which states only play the part of "authorized agents," or sometimes of "unauthorized agents," in the sense of holding good in civil law.

⊕

In our examination of the problem of intervention, we believe we have shown with sufficient clarity that both the external actions of a state and its internal relations are the concern of *all* other states; and as well, that there are circumstances in which those states have not only a right, but also a duty, to intervene in the external and internal affairs of another state. With this, however, collapses the doctrine of the two basic properties of state sovereignty: that of absolute autonomy in respect of its internal affairs (the so-called *souveraineté interne* of the state) and that of its absolute legal subjecthood in external affairs, i.e., in its relations with other states (the state's so-called *souveraineté externe* or *extérieure*). Now, the internal affairs of the state cannot in practice be separated from the external ones because these internal affairs represent for the most part only the preparatory stage of their external effects on international relations. This became all too clear with the foundation of the "Third Reich" (an alteration of the form of the state: an *internal* matter) and the assault that followed from this upon neighboring states (extortion and war: an *external* matter).

For this reason (and for the reasons given above from law, reason, and ethics), the absolute internal autonomy of states can no longer be countenanced. And the same goes for the absolute legal subjecthood of states in their international relations. Legal subjecthood includes two attributes: *freedom* and *equality*. In the context of the subjecthood of states, "freedom" means the reciprocal independence of states from each other, and "equality" means the right to the same degree of freedom as other states and the duty to respect that same degree of freedom in other states. The presence of these two attributes makes the state a *person* in international law—which raises the question of whether and to what extent this "person" is a reality. In order to be a reality, it must be *capable of acting*: of carrying out business and of infringing statutes. That is, it must possess a *unified will*, a will that can be justified and obligated by means of explicit declarations and conclusive actions. If it is to possess a will, and to express that will, however, a state cannot be an abstraction, or a legal relationship, or a thing. It must be traced back to *human* persons, since the latter alone are capable of being subjects of law.

Now, of the three constituents of the state (people, government, and territory), *territory* is immediately excluded from the possibility of legal subjecthood, as it is an object lacking a will. And so, only *people* and *government* remain to be considered. The relationship of these two groups produces the "will of the state," that is, the state's capacity to act as a subject of international law. This relationship, however, can be of three kinds. The government (or the governing sovereign) can: (1) rule on the basis of paterfamilias or *patriarchal* authority as *persona sui juris* ["person in one's own right"], ruling over the people considered as *persona*

94

aliena juris ["person subject to another"]; (2) stand toward the people as an appointed *guardian* to his ward; or (3) stand as the *representative* of the people, like the manager of a business in relation to the owners of that business.

PATRIARCH. The *patriarchal* relationship of ruler to ruled, based on the principle of *legitimism*, has today ceased to exist in all civilized states. Even where it formally continues (for example in Japan), it has changed to the (usually) great extent that the government has effectively renounced its power in favor of the people.

GUARDIAN. The relationship of a *guardian* to his ward is only seen nowadays in mandated territories,[26] where the government has been replaced by other states or by the League of Nations. Individual dictatorships might make a claim to this relationship by declaring that their dictatorship is a guardianship of the people (which is to last until the people (or relationships) are "mature" enough to bear the rights and duties of sovereignty themselves), but the governments of such states refrain from such declarations for political reasons and prefer to represent themselves as democratic, and to conceal the fact of their dictatorial power. This is the case in the Soviet Union today [mid-1940s], for example, which is governed as a dictatorship in its internal affairs, but for the most part enjoys describing itself as the "people's government of a free people."

REPRESENTATIVE. The third relationship, that of the *representation* of the people by a government appointed by the

[26] Cf. Oxford English Dictionary: "Mandated, *adj.*," 2. "Of a territory: assigned to the authority or protection of a particular power under a mandate of the League of Nations. Now *historical.*" ED

people, is present in all genuinely democratic states. Only genuinely democratic states are full "states," in the same sense that only a person who has reached maturity, or attained majority, is a full "person." In such full states there is present a structural possibility that the will of the people can be in accord with the will of the government—the possibility, that is, of the *actual* existence of a "will of the state" that is at all capable of action. But this accord of the will of the people with the will of the government is not produced by the will of the people following the will of the government, but by the expressed, agreed, supposed, or retrospectively approved will of the people determining the will of the government. It is in principle up to the will of the people to *decide* everything with which the life of the state is concerned. From this it follows, however, that the *actual* will of the state (the "subject" of international law) is the collective will of the people, i.e., of a resident group of people. This collective will is the expression of the ability of the individuals who make up a group settled in a given territory (the "people") to take decisions.

⊕

The primary capacity for law and for legal activity within the domain of international law (as within all domains of law whatsoever) rests, therefore, with the individual people. The human corporation of the "state" receives its capacity for law and for action from the individual people—from whom *alone* it is borrowed. The subjecthood of the state in international law is the capacity for law and for action that is awarded to it and delegated to it by individual people.

Why precisely *these* people organized themselves into a state, i.e., why they gave up a portion of their rights for the benefit of the community, and why their heirs and successors have agreed to this act of their predecessors and ancestors, is a question in itself. Earlier (from the point of view of the relative cultural missions of states) we discussed states as being one-sided, gradual revelations of the *idea* of law on the path to the *ideal* of law. Here, however, all that matters is that, from the legal standpoint, the state borrows its legal subjecthood from the individual people, *even* when the state is constituted by other states. Even when the recognition that is a necessary formal counterpart to substantive legal subjecthood takes place by means of other states, it nevertheless takes place *as* the expression of the will of a number of groups of people towards another group of people.

⊕

According to the conception that has prevailed up till the present day, individual people are *not* subjects, but only objects, of international law, since international law grants rights to and imposes obligations upon *states*, not on individual people. But am I then, as the captain of a ship, or even as a sailor on that ship, not an individual person when I am justified in taking, or am obliged to take, a particular action under international law? Yes, it can be countered, you are indeed justified, as an individual person, in behaving, and being obliged to behave, in a particular way. However, you are not *directly* justified and obliged by the community of states, but only *indirectly* through your *own* state. It is solely the latter that justifies and obliges you, *not* the international legal community.

Now, this objection could be countered by the argument from healthy common sense: if my state (i.e., all the individuals who belong to my state) is obligated by international law, then as an individual person it is by international law that I myself am really obligated, since international law not only obligates all the individuals who make up my state, but, for their part, those individuals also obligate me as *individuals*.

This view that the state only comes into consideration as a *representative* of those individuals belonging to it, whereas the latter are the *actual* subjects of international law, is not new (like most of those views we have argued for here). A number of authors, such as Baumgarten, Scelle, Stowell, Westlake,[27] Kaufmann, and not least the exponents of the influential Austrian school of pure jurisprudence (for example, Kelsen), insist on the standpoint that individual people *are* subjects of international law. Thus, Kelsen says the following on the problem discussed above:

> If, however, for example, those statutes of international law that concern the right to blockade confer the right to a particular line of conduct towards *members* of neutral states, and if those norms of international law that regulate war on land entitle the state waging war to a particular line of conduct towards the *civilian population*—and thus, necessarily, if these statutes, conversely, also obligate members of neutral or hostile states to a particular line of conduct towards the blockaded country or towards states waging war on land (and thus, in this case, persons are obligated under international law without any longer being regarded as "instruments of the state" in the usual more narrow sense of those

---

[27] Westlake, *Collected Papers,* xix, 1–2, 266, 498–503, 617–18.

words), then it is no longer easy to defend the assertion that international law applies only to states. It is a breach of international law if private persons violate the blockade; it is a breach of international law if private persons act as guerrilla fighters against armies in combat. Therefore it must be these private persons who are obligated under international law.[28]

People are the subjects of international law. And since international law is not limited to one group of people, but in principle applies to *all* people, international law is both formally and materially a right or law of *humankind*. In contrast to international law, the law of states is a *particular* law, a law that may not contradict international law, and that in cases of doubt must give way to international law. It is self-evident, then, that international law as a right of humankind has primacy over internal state law.

International law as a right of humankind is related to the law of an individual state as the universal is to the particular. That is, international law represents the fundamental basis for the law of individual states. It follows, conversely, that states do *not* possess absolute sovereignty. In sum, international law as a right of humankind, and the instruments of that law, are ranked *higher* than the states.

⊕

The insight that individual people are in truth subjects of international law is not merely persuasive in its content, but proves fruitful as well for the solution of many difficult

---

[28] Hans Kelsen, *Das Problem der Souveranität und die Theorie des Völkerrechts* (Tübingen, 1920), 165.

problems that otherwise cannot be solved. Among these problems is the contradiction that obtains between the *principle* of the equality of all states and the *fact* of their inequality in the rights and duties belonging to the so-called "great powers" when compared with the other sovereign states. Now, if the state is understood as a corporation, where it is not in the first place a question of the corporation as such but of the *people* belonging to the corporation (if, that is, one recognizes that individual people can be subjects under international law), then this contradiction equality and inequality of status is solved. For then it is a matter of the *portions* of *humanity* that are more important, both quantitatively and in terms of the quality of their culture. Luxembourg and France may well be equal before the *existing* statutes and regulations of international law (just as a private person is also equal to France under those statutes and regulations), but there is nonetheless an inequality between them when it comes to the *degree* of their participation in the *formation* of these laws and regulations, as well as when it comes to their interest in *participating* in the world-organization. For the portion of humanity described as "France" is more significant than the portion described as "Luxembourg." It is obvious that Russia, the United States, Great Britain, and China (which according to the principle of equality in the absolute sovereignty of states are *only* four subjects of international law alongside the fifty-nine or so other equally valuable and equally entitled subjects) represent the interests of humanity as a whole to a far greater extent than do, for example, Lithuania, Latvia, Estonia, and Finland, just because they *are* a greater portion of humanity than those other nations.

A state that represents a larger portion of the Christian

and civilized world[29] ought, self-evidently, to carry more weight in all the concerns of the international legislature, organization, and administration than a state that either represents a smaller portion of humanity or is culturally backward. Of course, a state cannot itself determine whether it is culturally backward or not. This must be done by the common judgment of the whole human cultural community, the family of cultured states. It may even happen that a state, or a group of states, drops out temporarily from the circle of culture, just as persons who are in themselves cultured and decent can fall ill psychologically and cannot be received into society while they are undergoing a manic episode. This in fact was exactly the case with Hitler's Germany. It could not be seen as, or treated as, part of the Christian and civilized portion of humankind because its behavior offended against everything essential to Christian civilization—even though, for its own part, it surely valued *itself* more highly than everything and everyone else. The common judgment of the human cultural community in this case was unambiguous. Indeed, the fact that taking up arms against Hitler's Germany was the only way of treating it that was considered possible ("unconditional surrender") already contains the judgment that Hitler's Germany could not be a cultural partner with which there could be a common level on which to undertake discussion and action.

---

[29] We say "Christian and civilized" because it cannot be a matter of a bare majority quantitatively; the majority must meet *two* requirements: it must be *qualitatively* (i.e., culturally) of high standing; and, quantitatively, it must represent the wills of many people. VT

It would be a crying injustice (and therefore also unlawful) if, for example, the tiny republic of San Marino and Italy were accorded equal influence on the make-up of the world-organization, its legislation, and its administration—for Italy in this context signifies the representation of a portion of humanity that counts over forty million legal subjects, while for its part San Marino represents only a few thousand. It would be patently unlawful, moreover, if the Holy See and Italy were seen as and treated as equally entitled, for the Holy See represents in a certain respect a portion of humanity numbering more than three hundred million, while Italy (even were its whole population to be in schism or to fall victim to heresy or apostasy) could only be in a position to represent, at most, forty million in that same respect. On the other hand, it would quite definitely also be unlawful to regard Holland and Abyssinia as having the same positive entitlements simply because their population counts are roughly the same. Although the cultural state of Holland represents roughly the same portion of humanity as does Abyssinia, that portion stands higher culturally. That is, since Holland has participated more in the cultural life of humanity, it must also be more important *to* humanity that Holland be granted a measure of rights that would enable it to influence this cultural life to a greater degree than would be right and proper in respect of Abyssinia.

⊕

The insight that individual people are in truth subjects of international law also helps solve the problem of what one might call the "penal" division of international law. It does so just as naturally as it helped solve the problem of the equality or inequality of states. The problem we speak of is that of those states guilty of breaches of international law, and in particular the most serious of such breaches: *war crimes*.

Let us imagine that a *state* has begun a war of aggression.[30] Under international law this is a case of a crime, equivalent to an assassination attempt upon a private person. As with any crime, it presupposes an *agent*, the person guilty of the crime. But who is the agent, who is the guilty "person" in the crime of "war"? If we hold fast to the theory of the sovereignty of states, believing that states alone are the subjects of international law and consequently also subjects of breaches of that law (i.e., are guilty of breaking international law), we are obliged to see states alone as the guilty parties, and *not* individual people (whether individually or in their sum-total, in peoples, or in governments). To be consistent, we would then also have to impose the legal consequences of the breach of international law (compensation, reparations, punishment) on a corporate "legal person" rather than on the individual people who had brought the breach about, for only this corporate legal person would be capable of breaching international law, given that it alone would be the subject of international law. Corporate liability to punishment, however, has been rejected as a matter of principle since the end of the eighteenth century, both in Roman law and in legislation and jurisprudence. The guilty *individuals*, and only they, are liable under the criminal law. *Societas delinquere non potest.*[31] The state as a

---

[30] War as a *human* crime will be discussed below.
[31] "Corporations cannot commit a crime." ED

corporation (a corporate "legal person") cannot be guilty of a crime, and that for the simple reason that it is not a *real* person under international law, but a *societas*, a community of *real* persons.

Thus, we find ourselves once again forced back onto the view that individual *people* are the subjects of international law, and that they *alone* can be guilty of breaches of international law, and be punishable for them. In practice, this view also leads to much more just consequences. Let one example suffice. In the war[32] of which the state of Germany is without doubt the original author, the state of Holland is innocent (or, at most, guilty of negligence). Now, there are many people in Germany (for example, all the Jews, many Catholics, and many members of other Christian denominations, as well as members of the idealistic intelligentsia) who not only have nothing in common with the groups of people who are war criminals or with their ideology, but are themselves also the direct *victims* of it. Conversely, there is in Holland (a state guiltless of the war) a well-organized and quite substantial movement that is at one ideologically, politically, and militarily with the German war criminals. Ought, then, the *whole* German people to be punished because the German state, as a "legal subject," is guilty? And ought the *whole* Dutch people go unpunished because the Dutch state, as a "legal subject," is guiltless? If, however, we understand individual people to be the *real* subjects of international law, and thus the only possible bearers of the consequences of breaches of that law, then we are dealing with people in considering the question of guilt and the

[32] The Second World War. ED

104

connected question of punishment—people who are equally guilty and equally punishable in any country, but who in another given case are equally innocent and equally exempt from punishment. On the one hand, there appear before the bench, side-by-side with Hitler, the Norwegian Quisling, the Dutchman Mussert, the Belgian Dégrelle, the Frenchman Laval, the Italian Mussolini, and so on; on the other, it is a matter of helping the innocent victims and granting them their rights (wherever it is not too late), not only in Norway, Holland, France, Belgium, Italy, and so on, but also in Germany itself.

The motto of the Allies to the effect that "the war is not being waged against the German people but against National Socialism" already embraces a conception of international law holding that individual people are guilty, which means that they are capable of breaches, and further, that they are subjects of international law.

Finally, it will be enough to mention that *without* the view that human beings are subjects of international law there is no real, logical basis for the fact of the recognition of rebels as a party waging war, for humanitarian intervention (indeed for intervention of any kind), or for interposition (intervention on behalf of certain members of a state).

In conclusion, let us summarize the arguments of this fourth section of our study by offering the following formulations:

International law is not the law of states, but a right of humankind. The true subjects of international law are human beings; states are only the representatives of those human beings' interests. International law outranks the law of particular states; it trumps the law of any and all states. International law is itself, however, subordinate to natural law, while natural law is itself subordinate to divine law.

3

The *Historical Foundations* of International Law as a Right of Humankind

I. The Historical Beginnings of International Law

ince the present study is underpinned by a method of considering international law that treats it as an organically inseparable part of universal human culture, the *history* of international law receives here a greater significance than is allowed it in many works on international law. Our concern is not merely to offer a description of the way today's international law has come into being, but also to gain insight into the nature of the firm and unshakable foundations of international law by observing it *unfold* in the course of the biography of humanity. It is a matter here of the foundations of international law. And history is precisely one of the areas where these foundations are most clearly manifested.

These foundations manifest themselves in history in two sorts of ways: (1) as having an *ordering* effect (when they are actually in force) upon the community of nations, an effect that works against chaos and protects against disaster; or (2) in *disordered*, cataclysmic, chaotic relationships within the same community of nations (when and insofar as the foundations of international law are not in force). These foundations are revealed whenever two groups of people organized into states interact with each other without using the means of force. In other words:

> The phenomenon of peace among nations that interact with each other is historically the archetypal phenomenon of international law.

If two independent, politically-organized nations are in a state of peaceful economic, political, and cultural interaction, the *reality* of international law is present. Peace (i.e., ordered relationships in the interaction between nations) is the *effect* of international law, regardless whether or not it is codified, whether it has this effect as so-called common law, or whether it appears in the form of treaties. Peace is simply *present* whenever nations interacting with each other are *not* at war with each other. International law is the organism of those norms without which interaction among nations is inconceivable, if that interaction is not to cease or be replaced by the use of force (war).

⊕

The objection that a law of *warfare* is also a part of international law (and that consequently international peace is not the *only* form in which international law can appear to be in force) collapses when we consider that war displays many *stages* on the way to becoming total war. To the extent that war does *not* consist in all the members of a nation (men, women, children, the elderly) killing everywhere and by any means all the members of another nation, it is not *total* war; that is, it still bears many of the features of the realm of peace. In principle, the regular peaceful *order* remains partially intact in time of war; and this persisting remnant of

108

"peace within war" is precisely the "law of warfare" within international law.

The norms of international law extend beyond their actual domain (which is peace) into war to the extent that war has not yet reached the stage of *total* war. International law is identical with the peaceful order of the international community. For this reason, it remains present during war also, in the norm that limits war and preserves the greatest degree of peace.

If it is objected that the statutes of the law of warfare (concerning, for example, the treatment of prisoners of war, the rules of *occupatio bellica*, and so on) are different in their content from the statutes that govern peaceful interaction—since they concern relations that *only* obtain in time of war—this can be answered by pointing out that only the *principles* of international law as the peaceful order of humankind can also be applied to warfare. This application leads of course to different *particular* statutes than would the application of the same principles to, for example, the domain of international trade. If, then, the question of the historical origin of international law is to be answered, it would have to be traced back to the following question: "Where and when did the actual situation of peaceful inter-action between two or more groups of people organized into states first occur?" For there has always been international law in every age (whatever its form, whether implicit or explicit) wherever there has been peace between two nations interacting with each other.

Thus, international law as a right of humankind (that is, as the "trans-state" order of peace) is from time immemorial. It is as old as peace itself. If explicit treaties under international law go back at least five thousand years (given that we possess a written treaty from the fourth millennium before Christ, whose parties are King Entemena of Lagash and the King of Umma),[1] how much older might a silently practiced, "customary" international law be? Or more correctly, how much older might a "natural" international law be?

The *temporal* "beginnings" of international law as an order of peace are, in any case, to be sought so far back in the past that for our purposes it is needless to ask about them. For these purposes, it suffices to establish that there always was some kind of international law wherever there was any kind of peaceful interaction between nations.

II. The *Divine Law* and *Natural Law* Principles of International Law, as Known from Historical Facts

EQUAL RIGHTS. As an archetypal phenomenon of international law, the *fact* of peaceful interaction between nations independent of each other contains in itself, as a kind of "consistent theme" of the groups of people in question, some convictions about matters of principle. For just as two people who interact with each other peacefully express the conviction that each of them has the *right* to demand of the other that he should himself be treated as he treats the other person (and conversely, that each has the *duty* to treat the other as he would like to be treated himself), so the fact of peaceful interaction between two or more nations is underpinned by this same conviction. Whatever else may have been explicitly agreed upon, the assumption of *equal rights*

---

[1] The treaty sets the border between the two states and appoints the king of a neighboring state as arbiter. M.J. Rostovsieff, in Walsh, *The History and Nature of International Relations* (New York, 1922), 41.

is always valid—the assumption, that is, of legal equality (*Gleichheit, égalité*). This assumption receives the ethical description of "justice" when it is applied in practice as a guideline. Correlatively, a given line of conduct is deprecated as "unjust" if it grants to one party a right to claims which that party denies to the other—that is, it is unjust if the assumption of equal justice is not applied. The fact of peaceful international interaction, then, is underpinned by the principle of equal rights, or fairness.

RELIABILITY. Another principle, this time underlying international commerce, consists in the fact that, given the same (or analogous) situation, it is to be expected that the parties will behave today as they behaved yesterday; or even that an explicit treaty will be adhered to (fidelity to treaties: *pacta sunt servanda*). It does not suffice for peaceful interaction that two parties should consider each other as having equal rights, since equal rights could also be understood in a *negative* sense (that is, as equal disadvantages). There must be in addition a commitment in the *positive* sense (i.e., to equally favorable treatment). As we have said, peaceful interaction presupposes a degree of certainty that the parties will behave tomorrow as they are behaving today, i.e., that they are *reliable*. Reliability, fidelity to treaties, is just as fundamental a constituent of peace as are equal rights.

TOLERANCE. Both equal rights and reliability, however, presuppose a third principle, without which neither equal rights nor reliability would be conceivable. This is the principle of mutual acceptance, of *tolerance* towards the divergent cultural, national, and social qualities of the parties concerned. A certain degree of tolerance (a degree that in the practice of diplomatic interaction is contained in the act by which one state recognizes another) is required *in order to* treat the other party as having equal rights and to see them as reliable. This degree of tolerance must be sufficiently great to sustain mutual commerce without the use of coercion, or intervention with the use of force. For example, the Arab caliphates were able to expand as far as the Pyrenees in the West and as far as central Asia in the East, not because the Arabs needed this much space, but because the caliphate behaved towards neighboring peoples of different faiths than their own in a way that was *intolerant* as a matter of principle. Thus, there came about a series of wars that proved successful for the Arab side. The principled intolerance of the Islamic empire during the period of its rise permitted no peaceful commerce with neighboring states. For this empire, a neighboring state did *not* have equal rights, and could thus not be a valid partner in a treaty—precisely because that state's mode of existence was not tolerated.

⊕

EQUAL RIGHTS, RELIABILITY, and TOLERANCE are the three principles of conduct (or, even, the convictions declared by means of conduct) without which it is impossible to imagine peaceful commerce between groups of people organized into states. They are, thus, the natural foundations of international law—the foundations without which international law (as an archetypal historical phenomenon in the peaceful commerce between states) would be inconceivable. These three principles are not a matter of happenstance; but they are, rather, rational consequences of a particular *worldview*.

EQUAL RIGHTS. For example, equal rights can be acknowledged only on the condition that a person or a group of people sees another person or another group of people (for example, the members of another nation) not as insubstantial shadows or as something absolutely alien, but precisely as *people* endowed with a soul just as they themselves are— that is, as *related* to them. The inner relatedness of human beings, when it is recognized despite all their differences, and when it is universalized and taken seriously, is the experience of the *brotherhood* of humankind, which in its turn points to a *common origin* of humankind.

RELIABILITY. Now, the common origin of humankind is one of the fundamental religious dogmas of human culture. Just as equal rights is a consequence of the religious teaching of the unity of the human race, so the principle of reliability is a consequence of the religious teaching that there is not only a natural world-order, but also a *moral* world-order that obligates human beings in their conduct just as much as the natural order determines it. The recognition of the presence of commitments of a higher kind than just those of natural law (i.e., commitments under divine law) is the root of reliability and of fidelity to treaties. A faculty of will that acknowledges no moral law higher than itself *cannot* be held to be reliable, since it does not know itself as bound to follow any higher commitment than that to its own advantage. Such a will, for example, is only able to remain faithful to a treaty for so long as that treaty is, or seems, advantageous to it. Thus, states ruled by groups of people or parties who propound materialistic or biological worldviews, or worldviews acknowledging no moral (i.e., divine) law higher than human beings themselves, cannot be partners to a treaty— since they are *unreliable*. That this is so, has been sufficiently demonstrated by historical experience.

TOLERANCE. Tolerance is also a rational consequence of a fundamental religious teaching. This is because the foundation for the acceptance of other ways and ideals than our own can only lie in the fact that we silently acknowledge a higher court of arbitration—i.e., that we do not believe that the verdict of greatest bearing lies with the parties themselves, but *above* them. The explicit basis for tolerance towards other people's ways and views is the belief that the final decision is up to God. So long as my neighbor does not indubitably (by virtue of any behavior, action, or want of action on his part) violate humanity with respect to myself or another, I do not intervene. Instead, I tolerate his way of life and of thinking, however different they may be from my own, since the final decision about their value and truth is not up to me, but to the source of all value and all truth: God.

The religious view that "God is the judge" thus underpins the tolerance that makes peaceful commerce between differently constituted groups of people possible. If it is objected that the fact of acceptance of divergent ideas and ways of life would be better described as *indifference*, we would answer by pointing out that in the present case it is a question of a tolerance practiced in the *commerce* of differently constituted groups of people with each other. Commerce, however, means an interaction: an interaction that leads either to a coming-apart (and so to the end of commerce) or to a peaceful continuation (and so, precisely, to the practice of tolerance). In *practice*, however, tolerance can never be an expression of indifference, precisely because it is *practiced*; that is, because it is put to the test in immediate encounters among divergent or opposed ways of life and of thinking.

Present, then, in the archetypal phenomenon of international law (that is, peaceful international commerce), are these three *principles*: equal rights, reliability, and tolerance. They are rooted, in turn, in three religious *beliefs*: the brotherhood of humankind, the divine law, and God's judgment, which is to say that they are rooted in belief in the triad of:

a common Father (God as the *creator*);
a divine guidance for the world (God as a *lawgiver*);
a highest court of judgment (God as *judge*).

⊕

What we have discovered through our substantive investigation of the historical *fact* of peaceful commerce between nations is that, in seeking its *principial* "beginnings" we find confirmed also its *temporal* beginnings, its origin in history. In other words, if *in principle* a religious and sacred content underpins peaceful commerce between nations, then the *historically* demonstrable origin of all law (and thus of international law too) is *also* to be found in the religious and sacred—that is, in divine law. For example, the *Manava-Dharma-Shastra*, also known as the *Laws of Manu*, was for the ancient Indians[2] both a religious and a juridical primal source, in which the process of the emergence of legal norms from the sacred element can be palpably sensed.

The process of the emergence and crystallization of legal norms from the sacred and religious element stands before our eyes no less clearly in these ancient Indian sources than it does in the Old Testament (especially in Deuteronomy,

---

[2] Philological research places the work's origin at about 100 BC, but the content of the original source is universally acknowledged to date from immemorial antiquity. Cf. Wegner, *Geschichte des Völkerrechts*, I.6.

the fifth book of the Pentateuch), in the *Zend Avesta* of ancient Iran, and in the *Laws of Hammurabi* from ancient Babylon. In all these primal sources, the fact of the original unity of the law as such is revealed—the fact, that is, of the unity of the norms of law, ethical life, and religion.

Now, "Thou shalt not kill" is found in the Decalogue alongside "Remember the sabbath day, to keep it holy"; and both commandments have a legal, ethical, and religious significance.[3] For if killing is a sin as well as a crime, the failure to observe the sabbath is also a crime as well as a sin. If we emphasize the *criminality* (illegality) of human violations of this command, it becomes a matter of *law*; if we emphasize the *sin*, the violation of *God's* law, it becomes an ethical and religious norm. Law emerges by means of the emphasis upon, and the separation of, particular parts of these universal sacred commitments as a sort of crystallization from a fluid solution saturated with content.

The *Laws of Manu*, for example, which is a religious book throughout, also contains provisions regarding "international law"—particularly those determining the law of warfare.[4] Now, these provisions (the sparing of peasants in military actions, the prohibition of poisoned weapons, the sparing of the undefended and unarmed) are at the same time religious and ethical precepts.

The *Laws of Manu* is a religious book; in it, the limits of the law of combat are often set by sacred ideas. It

---

[3] Both commandments have left a purely juridical residue in today's penal code. (VT) A related, in-depth treatment of the Decalogue may be found in the author's later (1972) *Proclamation on Sinai: Covenant and Commandments* (Brooklyn, NY: Angelico Press, 2022). ED

[4] *Manu* VII.90–93, cited in Wegner, *Handbuch des Völkerrechts.*

may nevertheless not be without significance that the practical results of these ideas amount to the same thing as the modern rules of international law deriving from many different thinkers.[5]

And it is indeed also not "without significance" that the *Laws of Manu* furnishes another example of how law emerges from religion. Once law *has* emerged, however, it can be taken hold of and treated on its own terms. A theoretical superstructure that "explains" or "grounds" it in a different way can even be added to it retrospectively. But if law is practiced in a manner so detached from the religious element[6] as to be considered and treated as *natural law* (i.e., as the commands of *reason* rather than of religion), there is nonetheless much still adhering to it that recalls its sacred origin. Thus Emil Seckel says that Roman international law

> retains . . . its sacred character throughout the whole course of its development, in particular in the law of warfare and of peace treaties. There was no closer community of so-called civilized states that could have developed a secular international law. Over the circle of all *gentes* [nations], only the gods presided. The invocation of the *foedera* [federation] is only meaningful in a situation where it was universally believed that the gods of foreign nations were also "just" gods, and that they would not let the breaking of an oath go unpunished, because the breach made by those who

---

[5] Ibid., I.3.7.

[6] As, for example, Roman law, which had its origin in the college of priests, but very soon began to function as a *law of reason*—as the Praetorian *jus gentium*, as a law *quod naturalis ratio inter omnes homines constituit*, i.e., as natural law.

worshiped them was committed at the expense of the worshipers of another group of gods.[7]

The Greek law of warfare, and of peace, too, with its Amphyctionians (which were at first leagues for the protection of particular shrines), provides at least as much evidence as does Roman law for the thesis that international law emerged from religion. Let us refer here only to the work of C. Phillipson,[8] where compelling evidence is to be found. What is at stake here (in connection with the task of shedding light on the foundations of international law) is simply to show in general that the historical beginnings of international law are of a religious kind, as is the case also with the essential content of the archetypal historical phenomenon[9] of international law: that is, the fact of peaceful commerce among nations. The beginnings in *time* and the beginnings *in principle* are, in *essence*, in accord with each other. In other words, what originated *temporally* from religion also carries the religious element in its deeper layers as its essential core.

[7] "Über Krieg und Recht in Rom," speech given on January 27, 1915. *Berliner Universitätsreden*, 47.

[8] Coleman Phillipson, *The International Law and Custom of Ancient Greece and Rome* (London, 1911).

[9] In the Roman period and in the Middle Ages, international law was traditionally (a tradition in which Hugo Grotius also joined by calling his *magnum opus* of international law *De juri belli ac pacis libri tres*) described as *jus belli ac pacis*, i.e., the thought was thus expressed that international law related to the tension between the phenomena of war and peace.

III. Fundamental Characteristics of the History of *Positive* International Law

The *principles* of international law expounded above (which are visible from history) are in their essence immutable. But they make their appearance as phenomena in different ways at different times in the changing shape of *positive* international law. These changes are of significance for us insofar as they reveal the changes undergone by the *concepts* of international law (illustrating thereby how views of international law alter with the changing times). These changing views also belong to the foundations (even if relative) of international law. They belong in particular to its *conceptual* foundations, as distinct from its *ideational* and *idealistic* foundations. In the Platonic sense, these changing views of positive international law represent the mutable *doxa* (in contrast to *dianoia* and *episteme*), i.e., *opinion*. It is a question here, then, of the basic characteristics of the history of "international legal opinion"; that is, of the concepts of how to set up a peaceful order that will *in principle* embrace all humankind. Now, as we have seen, these are the very concepts that make their appearance in the various orders of *positive* law in humankind's history. And so, it is to this historical dimension that we now turn.

INTERNATIONAL LEGAL ORDER AS *World-Organization*. The earliest historically demonstrable conception of this kind was that of the *world monarchy*, i.e., the unification of humanity under *one* rule. The *imperium* of the Romans was the inheritor of the "idea" of the Assyrio-Babylonian world monarchy, of the Median and Persian world monarchy, and of the world monarchy of Alexander the Great. The *pax romana*—as the result of empire—represented the fourth iteration or stage of the attempt to comprehend all human-kind in a *single* state. This stage was distinguished from its predecessors in particular by placing at its very center the idea of a universal *legal order*. The Roman imperium was an imperium of Roman law and Roman justice. Alexander the Great's empire, by contrast, rested more on an idea of universal *culture*. What it had at stake was to make Hellenistic culture universally valid. Thus, Alexander's campaign of conquest actually came about in consequence of Hellenistic culture, which embraced the territories of the Diadochoi (that is, from the Balkans to Egypt, and from Greece to Persia). But Alexander created no single legal order to cover this territory. This task was reserved for Rome.

Still more remote from the idea of a common legal order was the ancient Persian world monarchy. In that monarchy there was no question either of a universal *legal order* or of a universal *culture*, but rather of a universal *obedience* (the obligation to render tribute and allegiance) to the will of *one* man. In the case of the Chaldaean (Assyrio-Babylonian) world empire it was essentially a question of universal *subjugation*. It differed from the Persian world monarchy in that, whereas the Persian ruler claimed to be the "king of kings," the Assyrio-Babylonian rulers were as little disposed to tolerate kings beneath them as they were to tolerate kings alongside them.

These four world empires represent the ladder of the transition from universal despotism (Babylon) through universal super-monarchy (Persia) and universal cultural monarchy (Macedonia) to the universal legal state (Rome). Since these empires included several nations (and were thus neither *factually* nor *in principle* national states, but rather were, or wished to be, universal states), they at the same time represented a ladder of the *conceptual* development towards an *order of humankind* as the realization of perpetual peace. For if there are many rulers, they come into conflict with each other. If, however, there is only one ruler over all the nations of the *orbis terrarum* at any given time, peace is secured.

The concept of *"one* ruling will over *all* nations" is the first concept of a world-organization that embraces the whole of humankind. It is the first stage of the realization of the idea of international law as a right or law of *humankind*. This concept later underwent a metamorphosis, since this one will of the ruler must be not only a will, but as well the bearer and the proponent of a universal *culture*. The ruler has not only to rule, but to serve also—and to serve a universal culture and education. This is the Hellenistic concept of the order of humankind. The Roman concept of the order of humankind rises instead to mastery over world law as the universal order of justice, which the ruler (or the ruling nation) must serve, just as much as those it has subjugated must serve.

⊕

Through the influence of Christianity, the Roman concept of the world empire as world law metamorphosed into the idea of the Holy Roman Empire, which would henceforth be not merely the bearer of the order of world *law* but also the guardian of the order of the world's *salvation*—that is, the Christian church. If the Roman Empire had to serve *justice*, it was the task of the Holy Roman Empire under Charlemagne to place the legal order of justice in the service of the *salvation of souls*. But this meant that the state was not an end in itself. It had to serve something that surpassed it. It was in the Holy Roman Empire that the three-stage legal order came into being:

the state as an order of *positive* law;

the state-and-the-church-within-it as an order of *natural* law;

the church-above-the state as an order of *divine* law.

On its own, the "secular" sword is state power: positive law. The cooperation and mutual relationship of the "secular" and "spiritual" swords of the state-and-the-church-within-it is the rational basis of justice: natural law. The key power, however, that stands higher than everything else, is divine law. Thus, originally the pope crowned the emperor. But *within* the state, pope and emperor were equal, each representing his own domain, although in purely political (secular) matters the emperor alone was the authority—so long as he did not violate the natural and divine order. As for the primacy of divine law, Eike von Repgow[10] expresses it succintly at the beginning of the *Sachsenspiegel*:

God left behind on earth two swords for the protection of Christianity: to the pope he gave the spiritual sword, and to the emperor, the temporal one. Now, the pope is also required to ride a white horse at the specified time, and on this occasion the emperor shall hold his stirrup so that the saddle will not slip. The meaning is this: Any resistance to the pope in a way that he cannot control by ecclesiastical jurisdiction needs to be compelled by the emperor and his use of secular law to

[10] Eike von Repgow, medieval administrator who compiled the *Sachsenspiegel*, a code of law, at the beginning of the thirteenth century. ED

obey the pope. So, too, shall the spiritual jurisdiction assist the secular power when necessary.[11]

It was not in the great Assyrio-Babylonian empire, or in the Persian world-empire, or in the empire of Alexander the Great, but in the Holy Roman Empire (built on the soil of the Roman Empire) that the foundations in international law of the later "Western Christian family of nations" were laid. The original *community* of nations grew out of the soil of Roman culture and Roman legal order in the light of the *one* Christian faith. From an *historical* point of view, this original community of nations is the fragmented Holy Roman Empire, whose parts, despite this fragmentation, have nonetheless retained so much in common from the time when they were a unity that they still form a single *family* of nations, an international legal community. From a *legal* point of view, the community of international law is the legal successor of the Holy Roman Empire, just as the latter was the legal successor of the Roman *imperium*.

The echo of this common past was the bond that held together the original community of international law as a community—the echo, that is, of the *one* legal order and the *one* faith. "As far as its historical origin is concerned, international law is the law of the 'Christian-European' states,"[12] that is, of the now independent parts of medieval "Christendom." This international legal community then spread beyond Europe: first in the year 1783, as the United States became a community, and then in the first decades of the nineteenth century in the newly-independent states of

[11] *The Saxon Mirror: A Sachsenspiegel of the Fourteenth Century*, trans. Maria Dobozy (Philadelphia: University of Pennsylvania Press, 1999), 68.
[12] Franz von Liszt, *Das Völkerrecht* (Berlin, 1915), 3.

South and Central America. Only in 1856 did the community of international law expand beyond the borders of *Christian* culture, when Turkey was received into the "Concert of Europe" (acts of the Congress of Paris, article 7).[13] Japan, too, opened its borders to international commerce at this time (1854) and regulated its legal position within the international legal community by means of a series of treaties. With the League of Nations (1919), this community expanded to take in almost all of humanity.

INTERNATIONAL LEGAL ORDER AS (EUROPEAN) *Balance of Power*. We have described the growth of the original community of international law (the "Concert of Europe"), which although it *accepted* new members remained essentially a continuation of the Holy Roman Empire.[14] However, following upon the partition of the Empire after the end of the eighteenth century, French sovereignty was gradually re-established by means of a *new* conception of European order that dissolved the "empire of Christendom": the principle of the "balance of power in Europe." This principle was particularly abetted in winning out in the end over that of "world-organization" by three French statesmen under Kings Henry IV and Louis XIII.

Sully (Maximilian de Béthune, duke of Sully, a minister of Henry IV), Richelieu, and Mazarin put forward the idea of the balance of power in Europe under the slogan "against Hapsburg preponderance, for a balance of power in Europe." The former idea of a unity in faith and in empire

---

[13] The "Concert of Europe" was an agreement among the European great powers to maintain the balance of power in Europe. ED

[14] Thus concluding the subsection "International Legal Order as World-Organization." ED

(which was represented by the Hapsburgs) had less and less of a claim to validity, especially because not only had the empire disintegrated into a collection of sovereign states, but the unity of faith had been destroyed as well by the Reformation. Thus, with the Treaty of Westphalia (1648), the "balance of power in Europe" (together with parity in religion) gradually grew into the ruling order of Christian and civilized humanity, becoming thereby the "order" of the now disintegrating Holy Roman Empire: a sort of continuation of the empire of Christianity, its "Diadochi era"[15] so to speak. This "Diadochi" situation of European humanity is universally understood, however, as the development of the modern international legal community.

> The international legal community rests on the collegial, not the sovereign, principle; it is not a state of states, but a federation of states, an association of sovereign states for a particular purpose.[16]

That is, positive international law is not a statute,[17] but a treaty. As a treaty, however, it presupposes parties to the treaty bearing equal rights. That is, up until the Second World War, the *plurality* of sovereign states is the presupposition of international law. With this, the transformation that the international legal order has undergone since the Carolingian age comes clearly into view: whereas it once stood under the sign of the vertical dimension of *public* legal

[15] The wars of the Diadochi (322–281 BC) were a series of conflicts fought between the generals ("Diadochi") of Alexander the Great over who would rule the empire following his death. ED

[16] Franz von Liszt, *Völkerrecht* (Berlin, 1915), §1, 7.

[17] A statute is a written law enacted by the legislative body of a state. In biblical usage, it is a law made by a sovereign, or by God. ED

subordination, it now (precisely with the recognition of the "balance of power in Europe") follows the horizontal dimension of contiguity with *private* law. The vertical, or hierarchical, principle was surrendered when Francis I of Austria abdicated his imperial title (in the remnants of the territories where it was still valid) on August 6, 1806. In force thereafter was only the international law of the politically individualistic ("private-law") community of states relying on actual practice and on treaties—all this on the legal and political foundation of the principle of the balance of power, first in Europe, then in the world as a whole.

After the Treaty of Westphalia there was certainly no lack of attempts to give up the principle of the balance of power and to unite Europe again by force under the leadership of a *single* power: Louis XIV, Napoleon, and Hitler attempted just this: to destroy the balance of power in Europe and arrogate leadership in Europe to themselves by force—or, as was the case with Louis XIV, by political means. These attempts, however, were not made on the same basis as that on which unity had once been realized (on the basis, that is, of Christian culture and the Roman tradition of order), but instead on the basis of the naked right of the stronger party.

Now, the right of the stronger party (which, tradition relates, was already championed by the sophist Callicles[18] in Athens) is *itself* an idea on which the idea of the balance

---

[18] "A pure materialist in his philosophical thought, Callicles concludes that law as it rules in Attic democracy is actually the opposite of law. For according to him, in this law the many weak had combined to fetter the few strong individuals in the bonds of law. Nature, however, he argued, taught . . . that in the course of nature the strong should triumph over the weak. Natural law, for him, is the power of the stronger party." H. Rommen, *Die ewige Wiederkehr des Naturrechts* (Leipzig, 1936), 21.

of power in Europe depends, and which it thus keeps alive. For the balance of power in Europe is underpinned by the presupposition that states are not *legal* unities but *power* unities. This is already clear in the language used: the *Great Powers*. Thus, in principle, *every* individual state poses a perpetual danger that it will overpower the other states. And so it is precisely to avert this danger that a balance of power is necessary. One state's becoming powerful is always to be either prevented or balanced out by means of special measures (building up armaments, alliances). The system of the balance of power among states is in essence an "organized mistrust" in which every state is considered to be a potential enemy of the others, and in which no treaties, declarations, or other legal agreements, but only power relations, are in the end decisive. The order of peace is only secured insofar and for so long as no state or alliance of states is in a position to overpower the other states: this is the *actual* content of the idea of the balance of power.

Given that the balance of power is based on actual power relations, it brings along with it both misgivings about existing power relations and the hope of altering them to one's own advantage. For if no *superordinate* ideal, no real and binding guarantee, is acknowledged as an inviolable foundation, so that in fact everything depends on power relations alone, why shouldn't states try to alter power relations to their advantage? Why shouldn't a state that happens (for political, economic, and military reasons) to find itself in a more favorable position than its neighbors exploit this advantage? Conversely, *in principle* the balance of power brings along with it (coupled with the abiding temptation to put power relations to the test) the necessity of a competitive arms race. For, since the idea of the balance of power is an idea of a balance of states as unities of *power*, each step in the direction of increased potential for war on the part of one state necessitates a corresponding step in the same direction on the part of the other states. Sooner or later, however, such a competitive arms race leads not only to ever-increasing tensions in the interaction between states (as well as to an intensifying mutual mistrust among their peoples), but also, necessarily, to a situation in which one state or group of states succeeds in achieving a real or supposed *lead* over the others. From this, however, there follows the only possible course of action for the state concerned: to make *use* of the lead that was achieved at such great cost, i.e., to extort advantage for itself either by coercion of another state or by making war upon it.

In principle, the system of the balance of power is a potential "war of all against all" (Epicurus, Hobbes). It is not an order of *peace* at all. It is nothing more than an order of *armed truce*. Peace does not mean merely the absence of military action (which is equally the case in an armed truce), but the absence of rational *causes* for a war. Such causes are never present, however, in an order that does not rest merely on power relations, but rises *higher* than individual states and *guarantees* law and justice. By contrast, the balance of power is by its nature a *continual* cause of war, since its presupposition and foundation is the principle of power.

⊕

For a thoughtful observer, what results from the content of the idea of the balance of power is confirmed by the facts of history. Has the system of the balance of power brought peace? The question must be answered with a decided negative. Louis XIV's wars (the campaigns against the Netherlands and the Empire; the War of the Spanish Succession); the Great Northern War; the Seven Years' War; the wars of Frederick the Great; the French revolutionary and Napoleonic wars; the Crimean War; the Austro-Prussian War (1866); the Franco-Prussian War (1870); the Russo-Turkish War; the Balkan War; the First World War; the war in Eastern Europe; the Second World War—this is a list of wars that, even though incomplete and confined to Europe, sufficiently demonstrates that over the course of the last two and a half centuries the "Concert of Europe" has oscillated between war and *armed truce*, not between war and *peace*. This is because, apart from two attempts to create an order of peace, the system of the balance of power in Europe remained in force after each war, and consequently bore the *causes* of a further war within itself. Moreover, this situation will last until the dogma of the absolutely sovereign state is abandoned, for a plurality of absolutely sovereign states can only exist in the form of a balance of power. *War and the unlimited sovereignty of states belong together.* The cul-de-sac into which the international legal community has got itself consists in the fact that, since it is founded on the unlimitedly sovereign state, it can survive only as a balance of power—a political order in principle always on the brink of war.

INTERNATIONAL LEGAL ORDER AS *Federation* OR *Alliance*. We can now see what is unsatisfactory about the system of the balance of power (and thus also about unlimited sovereignty) in the past and in the present. Large-scale attempts have twice been made to replace the "organized mistrust" of the balance of power with the "organized trust" of a federation. The first attempt was the so-called Holy Alliance of 1815, and the second was the League of Nations of 1919. At present [mid-1940s] we are living through a third attempt, the establishment of the United Nations (UN). Alongside the system of maintaining the fragmented successors of the empire of Christendom (the "family of nations") in a balance of power, there also emerged in 1815, with the Holy Alliance, an effort to gather this family of nations together on a *new basis*. In other words, after the centrifugal development could be considered complete, the search for a kind of *restoration* of unity made itself visible. By their nature, the Holy Alliance and the League of Nations, like the UN, are steps in the direction of a realization of a *civitas maxima*, an international legal order in which individual states cede *part* of their sovereignty to a trans-state authority and a trans-state organization. The West developed out of unity, and now (having experienced to the full the consequences of fragmentation) is striving to get back to unity.

As was said, the Holy Alliance represents the first step in this direction. It was indeed an attempt to once more unite the European community of nations into a *family* organized on patriarchal principles by means of an awareness of its Christian foundations. The second article of the Holy Alliance reads as follows (the emphases are the author's):

> In consequence, the sole principle of force, whether between the said Governments or between their Subjects, shall be that of doing each other reciprocal service, and of testifying by unalterable good will the mutual affection with which they ought to be animated, to consider themselves all as members of one and *the same Christian nation*; the three allied Princes

looking on themselves as merely designated by Providence to govern three branches of *the one family*, namely, Austria, Prussia, and Russia, thus confessing that the Christian world, of which they and their people form a part, has in reality no other Sovereign than Him to whom alone power really belongs, because in Him alone are found all the treasures of love, science, and infinite wisdom, that is to say, God, our Divine Savior, the Word of the Most High, the Word of Life.

It is therefore a question of the restoration of the relationship of *trust* that was severely shaken by the catastrophe of the French Revolution and Napoleonic imperialism. And the relationship of trust is to be grounded, in particular, on *Christianity*, so as to allow the unity of *Christendom* to become a reality once again by means of familial and fraternal alliance among its princes. Almost all European states joined the Alliance.[19] It was actually led, however (after France joined it in Aachen in 1818), by the pentarchy of the great powers: England, France, Austria, Prussia, and Russia. The great powers consulted among themselves on the common concerns of Europe at the Congresses of Aachen (1818), Troppau (1820), Laibach (1821), and Verona (1822). Despite changing relationships among the great powers (caused, in particular, by England's growing distance from the ideology and policies of the continental powers), the system of the Congress of Vienna prevailed until around 1848. Its inability to maintain itself thereafter is usually ascribed to its conservative ("reactionary") legitimist nature.

---

[19] Great Britain did not ratify it. The Holy See remained outside the Alliance.

According to this view, its conservative legitimism repelled liberal and progressive circles on one hand, and on the other forced the entire New World into open opposition[20]—indeed, impelled even England towards an essentially antagonistic stance.

Particularly unattractive was the practice of going beyond arbitration of any disputes that might surface and defending the "endangered" legitimate order by means of armed *intervention*. Thus, Austrian troops went into Naples and Sardinia in 1821, and French troops into Spain in 1823, in order to support the legitimate monarchies "in the name of" the Holy Alliance. The United States—which owed its own independence to a successful rebellion—could only view these interventions with mistrust and suspicion, especially as at that time a number of Central and South American states were coming into being along the path of revolution, and this process could not be made compatible with the principle of legitimacy prevailing in Europe. The principle of the French Revolution (the primacy of the people's will) had been overcome in Europe and replaced by the principle of legitimacy. This led to a division of the international legal

---

[20] President Monroe's message of December 2, 1823, states: "The political system of the allied powers is essentially different in this respect from that of America. This difference proceeds from that which exists in their respective Governments; and to the defense of our own, which has been achieved by the loss of so much blood and treasure, and matured by the wisdom of their most enlightened citizens, and under which we have enjoyed unexampled felicity, this whole nation is devoted. We owe it, therefore, to candor and to the amicable relations existing between the United States and those powers to declare that we should consider any attempt on their part to extend their system to any portion of this hemisphere as dangerous to our peace and safety."

community into two systems: the European system of legitimacy and the American system of the unlimited sovereignty of the will of the people.[21]

Are these reproaches against the system of legitimacy justified, if we want to judge the Holy Alliance with the help of the experience of the Second World War and the postwar period?

⊕

The Holy Alliance was not a theoretical edifice built overnight from scratch. It was an order formed in the wake of twenty-five years of bloody revolution and bloody wars as the expression and result of a complete victory over those subversive forces. After the Jacobins had set the "will of the people" (which means to say the will of their own party) above the ties of the religion of humanity and the right to fairness and justice; after Napoleon had made and unmade kingdoms by force; after, in other words, *order* as such had been attacked and shaken to its foundations—what principle should or *could* be selected and proclaimed in Europe as guide and lodestar, if not that of legitimacy and religion? For legitimacy, in connection with Christianity, is, after all, the natural law that knows itself to be connected to divine law, and that had been suppressed by revolutionary *rationalistic* natural law (which had been inaugurated by the Sophists). If the essence of this contrast consisted in the fact that,

---

[21] The so-called Monroe Doctrine has *two* sides: on one hand it means the mutual *non-mixing* of the two hemispheres, but on the other, the right of the American peoples—which follows from this—to frame their destiny according to their own judgment (i.e., the thesis of the French Revolution against legitimism).

to a natural law *rooted in divine law*, autonomous reason opposed its revolutionary "emancipated" natural law, how could it now have been possible to take this rationalistic natural law as a basis for order in Europe, given that a twenty-five-year-long struggle *against* this revolutionary natural law had been undertaken in the name of *Christian* natural law? Legitimacy and Christianity were the two highest values threatened and under attack. Their restoration was the *meaning* of the victory over subversion. They did triumph, and were restored as the highest values.

But might a *compromise* have been possible? Could a principle have been selected that held the "conservative" and the "progressive" in equilibrium? The subversive and revolutionary tendency had, however, first to be contained. If that had not been achieved—and that by means of the thirty years of the Holy Alliance—then ever further stages of revolution would have followed in uninterrupted succession. The French revolution was an alarmingly indicative stage of the great revolutionary current that began with the humanism of the fourteenth century and led via the Reformation to the Enlightenment of the eighteenth century, which "became flesh" in the revolution of 1789. From there it strode forward through 1830 and 1848 to the Paris Commune of 1871, and on to the Russian revolutions of 1905, February 1917, and October 1917. At the beginning of the revolutionary development stands a "harmless" humanism, with its enthusiasm for secular culture; at the end stands black and red Bolshevism as the final result of the destruction of the great temple of piety in which and from which the soul of the West draws its life.

⊕

Secular humanism's delight in thinking and investigating without God supplied the initial push in the direction of later "emancipations," by which we mean dissolutions of the bonds of *reverence*: reverence for the tradition of the Church, along with its saints and sages; reverence for the tradition of chivalry, with its respect for women and its sacred pledge and bond of honor; reverence, finally, for human beings themselves, with their right to life, freedom, and property. Secular humanism began by *thinking* without God; it ended by *living* without God. The impulse towards emancipation from *one* bond (enabling free investigation without regard to religion) led in the end to liberation from *all* bonds: the human being without reverence, the psychological Bolshevik (whether he appears as a black Bolshevik of the right, or as a red Fascist of the left, being immaterial). The human being without reverence has now arisen, and cannot be got rid of from the world.

This development was already recognizable at the outset of the nineteenth century. And it *was* recognized. Although Tsar Alexander I believed precisely in a Christian progress towards liberalism, and King Friedrich Wilhelm of Prussia pondered a fidelity to treaties guaranteed by the power of the Alliance, it was the much-derided Metternich who recognized the true extent of the danger it was the duty of the Alliance to avert. The high idealism of the Alliance was owed to Tsar Alexander. But to Metternich was owed the insight that the Alliance was indispensable to prevent European Christendom from being swept away for lack of reverence. A compromise would have been of no use. Indeed, it would have been actively damaging, for at that time (after many years of external war) it was a matter of opening up a front also in the cultural domain against any further progress on the part of subversion. This, however, could come about only through a clear recognition both of the principle of legitimacy and mutual trust among the allies in Christendom as a foundation. If it was hoped to restore and maintain *international* legal security by means of the force of respect for legitimacy, and to restore and maintain *universal* cultural security by means of the force of respect for the bonds of Christianity, it was as well the best *political realism* to build unambiguously, openly, and without compromise, on these forces.

Why, then, did the system of the Holy Alliance not endure longer than it did? For the same reason as in the case of the League of Nations in the present day [1947]: as now, so then, *good will* was lacking. However serviceable and good a system or an order may be, it depends in the final analysis on *people*—people who give up on it, relinquish it, reinterpret it, falsify it, or simply betray it. The number of (true or false) "guardians" of a system need not be large. A few dozen people can suffice to blow to pieces a universally recognized order. The great problem consists, not so much in what system one chooses and how one organizes the world, as in how and where one is to find *people* who are truly of good will, and whose intelligence can be brought to bear. In the end, it is a matter of *trust*. There is no system, whether internal to the state or international, that is so fashioned as to function without the substance of trust as its final, practical foundation. Even if there is a ten-step audit, there must nevertheless be as an *eleventh* step a trusted final auditing authority.

The system of the Holy Alliance did not "collapse" because it was fantastical or weak or morally unreliable *in itself,* but because, just like the League of Nations in our age, it was *betrayed.* The special interests of the nationalists, of the states, of classes, exercised their disintegrating influence on the Holy Alliance at that time in just the same way as happened when the League of Nations "collapsed." Instead of "special interests" working towards disintegration, one could equally well say that the "balance of power in Europe" mentality triumphed over the ideology of the Holy Alliance—just as in our age the "balance of power in the world" mentality has triumphed over the memory of the League of Nations, which is to say, over the significance of the family of humanity.

INTERNATIONAL LEGAL ORDER AS (world) *Balance of Power.* After the "collapse" of the Holy Alliance, as the system of the balance of power once again achieved unlimited domination (the Crimean War, the Austro-Prussian War, the Franco-German War, the Russo-Turkic War), and new groupings (the Triple Alliance versus the *Entente Cordiale*) were formed within this system, thereby announcing the approach of a major war by the gradual build-up of armaments, an attempt was made towards the end of the nineteenth century to do the best that was feasible: if not to avert the threat of catastrophe, then to limit it to the extent possible. At the invitation of the Russian Emperor (Nicholas II, text of August 24, 1898), a peace conference met on May 18, 1899, in the Hague. Twenty-six states were represented. Only the two Boer republics, the Central and South American states, and the Congo were absent. (The Holy See, too, was absent from the conference, since it was not invited.) The acts of the conference, subscribed on July 29, 1899, by all the powers represented at the conference, listed as the results of the proceedings the following:

Three conventions, (1) concerning the peaceful settlement of international disputes; (2) with respect to the laws and customs of war on land; and (3) for the adaptation to maritime warfare of the Geneva Convention of 1864.

Three declarations concerning the limitation of hostilities in war.

A unanimously adopted resolution: that "the restriction of military charges, which are at present a heavy burden on the world, is extremely desirable for the increase of the material and moral welfare of mankind."

Six wishes in relation to further consultation about a second peace conference.

On June 15, 1907, the second Hague peace conference met. This time, forty-four states were represented, since the states of Central and South America, which had not previously been invited, now took part. Absent were Lichtenstein, Monaco, San Marino, Honduras, Costa Rica, Korea, Afghanistan, the Congo, Abyssinia, Liberia, and Morocco. The Russian government's agenda included the revision of the three conventions of 1899, as well as maritime law. The results of the conference included thirteen conventions and a *declaration*, to the following effect:

- the peaceful settlement of international disputes;
- the limitation of the employment of force for the recovery of contract debts;
- relative to the opening of hostilities;
- laws and customs of war on land;

- rights and duties of neutral powers and persons in case of war on land;
- relative to the status of enemy merchant ships at the outbreak of hostilities;
- relative to the conversion of merchant ships into warships;
- relative to the laying of automatic submarine contact mines;
- concerning bombardment by naval forces in time of war;
- for the adaptation to maritime war of the principles of the Geneva convention;
- relative to certain restrictions with regard to the exercise of the right of capture in naval war;
- relative to the creation of an international crisis court;
- rights and duties of neutral powers in naval war;
- *declaration* prohibiting the discharge of projectiles and explosives from balloons.

In addition, the conference's final act also contained:

- a declaration in favor of compulsory arbitration;
- a renewal of the resolution reached in 1899 about the limitation of military charges;
- an expression of four wishes, namely:
  (a) concerning the creation of a Judicial Arbitration Court;
    (b) concerning the safeguarding of peaceful commerce in case of war;
    (c) the regulation of military charges of foreigners;
    (d) the legal regulation of maritime law.

On the last point, a special conference was held at which eight great powers, as well as Spain and the Netherlands, were represented. The proceedings lasted from December 4, 1908 until February 26, 1909. The result was a declaration on maritime law, contraband in war, unneutral service, the destruction of neutral prizes, transfer to a neutral flag, enemy character, convoy, compensation, resistance to search, and provisions on blockade in time of war.[22]

⊕

As can be seen from the above, the overall picture of the Hague peace process shows that, when compared with the spirit of the Congress of Vienna, the idea of a world peace organization had been abandoned, and that out of this spirit of resignation an effort was being made to at least hold back the coming war, and to postpone it by means of arbitration. In the case of both of the two Hague conferences, and of the London conference on maritime war, what is really at stake is the law of *warfare*, i.e., the restriction and humanization of a war thought to be in itself unavoidable. Representatives of forty-four states came together and determined the rules of the *future* conduct of war (with the exception of arbitration, which was supposed to make the outbreak of war more difficult or to help to avoid it, and the desire to limit the build-up of armaments). The intention was indeed, as it always is when the law of warfare is made part of international law, to turn the war into a *minimal* war—to keep it as far as possible from total war, which is contrary to international law. But with what means? With those of the self-obligation of the states who

---

[22] Franz von Liszt, *Die Völkerrecht* (Berlin, 1915), §3:2,3.

explicitly held themselves bound by the law proclaimed. Thus the declaration of October 18, 1907 prohibiting the discharge of projectiles and explosives from balloons (which was not signed by Germany) stated:

> The Contracting Powers agree to prohibit, for a period extending to the close of the Third Peace Conference, the discharge of projectiles and explosives from balloons or by other new methods of a similar nature.

This modest proposal to wait for the next peace conference to throw projectiles from the air (was the next peace conference going to permit this in principle?) is, however, even restricted:

> The present Declaration is only binding on the Contracting Powers in the case of war between two or more of them. . . . In the event of one of the High Contracting Parties denouncing the present Declaration, such denunciation shall not take effect until a year after the notification. . . . This denunciation shall only have effect in regard to the notifying Power.

In other words, the Hague process shows *so little* faith in the good will of the governing circles of the states, that, foreseeing the use of a new method of waging war, it does not expect these circles to be able indefinitely to prohibit bomb attacks from the air. On the other hand, the dependence on the "unlimited sovereignty" of the individual states is *so great* that even this prohibition has an escape clause added to it. It seems to be more important not to violate the sovereignty of the states than it is to prevent a monstrous catastrophe from befalling humanity! When faced with a choice between limiting the total power of the state or bombing

141

from the air, a choice was made for the inviolability of the state's total power, and humanity is sacrificed to this choice.

⊕

Without doubt, the Hague peace process did much good towards the limitation and humanization of war. But it also illustrates how hopelessly deep-rooted was the "balance of power" mentality (with its *raison d'état*, total power of the unlimitedly sovereign state, state as the sole subject of international law, and community of states), which had led to a system of the balance of power among special interests in principle hostile to each other (arms races, war as the *ultima ratio* of international law) at the turn of the century and immediately before the 1914 war.

Just think how peculiar would be a conference between, let us say, respective citizens of a state, called for the purpose of regulating the use of armed force in family feuds, blood-revenge, and self-defence within the life of the state! Public penal law and civil courts have long since made it impossible to employ weapons as a means of settling private disputes. How does it come about, then, that the *same* people who within their own state turn to the courts to settle disputes, want nonetheless to employ weapons to settle disputes between their state and other states? The reason why the international order is so shamefully backward as compared with the interior legal order of states, is the damaging superstition that states have unlimited sovereignty. According to this superstition, the sovereignty of states is to be maintained by *any* means and at *all* costs, at the expense of any obligatory jurisdiction (over arbitration and punishment) among states, and thus at the expense of world peace—at the expense, that is, of disarmament, of the world economy, of a common struggle against poverty in the world, of the solution of social questions, and so on. *Pereat mundus, vivat status*: "let the world perish so long as the state can live."

Any progress in the area of international law as a right of humankind is held back by the damaging dogma of the unlimited sovereignty of the state. For as long as we continue to worship this idol, there will never be a true world legal order that secures peace.

⊕

Immediately before the First World War, this idol of the unlimited sovereignty of the state was at its zenith. In politics and in the theory and practice of international law it ruled quite without limit. Millions of people then died for its sake when world war broke out. There is a whole literature on the causes of the First World War. Both the political aspect (the opposition between the Triple Alliance and the *Entente Cordiale*, the assassination in Sarajevo, Austria's demands on Serbia, Russia's meddling, Germany's and France's meddling, the series of mobilizations, the series of declarations of war) and the question of blame for the last world war have been sufficiently discussed that one can now put the question afresh—not merely politically or legally or with reference to the question of blame, but the question *in itself*, namely: How did it come to world a war, and who in reality had an interest in its doing so?

If one asks this question against the background of the literature devoted to answering it, a remarkable result presents itself: immediately before the outbreak of the war, not a single country or a single nation was either disturbed or endangered in what it needed to subsist, and economically, there was a universal rise in the standard of living. Not only in Germany and in the West, but also in Russia, an unprecedented level of economic development was underway. There was no unemployment: Italian and Polish workers were working in the Ruhr region of Germany in the hundreds of thousands, German workers were employed in America, and Russia indicated inexhaustible possibilities of absorbing workers with special skills. Similarly, there was no overpopulation, no "*Lebensraum* problem," for all borders stood open to all, and everyone could seek and find the necessities of work and existence where they might prefer. World trade and world commerce were at a high. The currencies of all countries (the dollar, the pound, the ruble, the mark, the franc) were all stable and enjoyed general trust. The commercial network of the world was in the midst of rapid construction. International commodity trade showed a continually rising curve. In St. Petersburg in summer 1914 one could buy French perfumes, English woolens, Chinese silks, German medicines, Italian oranges, Turkish tobacco, Swedish furniture, Persian carpets, Greek confectionery, American cars, and so on, all at entirely reasonable prices. The same went for almost all the great cities of the world, since the system of customs controls for the purpose of absolute economic autarky had not yet been introduced (this system being, precisely, one of the results of the world war).

Furthermore, since the conditions of work, trade, and commerce were so favorable, social relations were also much better than in the post-war period—once again, not only in Germany or in Western Europe, but in Eastern Europe too. The general standard of living was higher everywhere before the war—and this was true also for the working class. If there was no *need* that caused the war—that is, no economic

144

The *Historical Foundations* of a Right of Humankind

need, no constraints on space, no unemployment, no lack of markets, no financial crises, no social crises—then it was *prosperity* itself that led to war. And it led to war particularly in the sense that it made possible an increasing potential for armament. In addition, as regards the system of the balance of power, the nations were disposed in two military alliances that were mutually hostile to each other. The Triple Alliance (Germany, Austria-Hungary, and Italy) and the *Entente Cordiale* (Russia and France, with a friendly England) had been preparing for two decades for an "eventual" war. For how long was one supposed to go on preparing? The shots rang out in Sarajevo. The Central Powers believed themselves militarily ready for war. War broke out.

⊕

The fact of the last world war shows, with as much clarity as could possibly be desired, how it is possible that although nations can lack the least occasion or cause for war (for they had nothing to gain, *only* something to lose), war can nevertheless break out—a war that sucks hundreds of millions of people into its vortex.

Culture, the economy, true patriotism, were not involved in the war. It was not about these. What, then, *could* have been the true cause of the war? It could only have been *one thing*: the absolutely sovereign state as a value *in itself* (i.e., without regard to nation, culture, or economy) within a system of rivalry (i.e., the "balance of power in Europe") among several equally absolute sovereign states.

"Militarism" does not happen by itself, any more than "imperialism" does. Both militarism and imperialism are necessary accompanying phenomena of *statism*—the mentality that regards the *state* as an absolute value. For if we

145

regard our state as an absolute value (i.e., if we value it "above everything else"), it must also be *strong* and *powerful*. In order to become strong, it must have a mighty army at its disposal. In order to become powerful, it must order its weaker neighbors around. Thus, militarism and imperialism result with inner necessity from the view that the state (i.e., *the* state, in each individual case) possesses so high a value that *everything else* is to be sacrificed to it.

The sacrifices that the state has demanded of humanity in order to reach its unreal goals exceed *by multiples* all the sacrifices ever made on behalf of religion, science, art, or social values. By how many multiples does the number of "martyrs" to the state (i.e., of people who have died for, been crippled for, or been made destitute for, the state) exceed that of the Church's martyrs? But is the state, as a *value*, *worth* this sacrifice? Does the Hegelian doctrine that the state is "the presence of God upon earth" rest upon truth? It is all too clear that the state has the tendency to be and to mean *everything*, i.e., to unite within itself the functions of order, education, and leadership. The totalitarian state— fascist or communist—wishes to take control of "the politics of religion," "the politics of culture," "the politics of the economy," "the politics of law." It wants to transform all these domains into "politics," so that culture is to become the *politics* of culture, and so on.

The liberal, minimal state, on the other hand, is the degree of organization necessary to create and maintain a legal order that *serves* the individual and *protects* his interests. Culture, the economy, and social and political relationships lie, in principle, outside the competence of the state. While the individual has to serve the maximal state, the minimal state serves the individual. The latter state is "minimal" in the sense that the individual ought only to notice the state to the extent that it is absolutely necessary to protect his freedom. The legislature, the executive, and the judiciary of a liberal, minimal state may only shape public life insofar as this is necessary to protect the "extra-state" (private) freedom of *all* individuals.

Now, given their freedom, one particular use that citizens of a liberal legal state can make of it is to commit themselves to the Christian religion and the Church. In *that* case the *state* must serve the *Church* just as it serves any other use of freedom made by its citizens. The liberal minimal state then becomes a *Christian* minimal state, that is, a legal order that *serves* Christianity. This legal order relates to the Church and to the whole of cultural life rather as the body relates to the soul. Just as the body serves the soul by providing the stage upon which consciousness develops, so the minimal Christian state serves the Christian culture championed and led by the Church. The functions of education, of setting cultural goals (leadership), of shaping social relationships (e.g., family life), are not incumbent upon such a state. The state authority has *only* to see to it that the respective corporations of cultural, economic, and social life are accorded their rights.

From this perspective, the state is a value that *follows upon* other values of cultural life. *Its* value, precisely, is that of a *legal order*—and no other. We should get rid of all the "mysticism" (e.g., messianism of the state and its "divine mission") with which the idea of the state has (for the most part obscurely) been embellished. It is nothing more than an association set up to fulfill a purpose—that of creating and maintaining a legal order. The state should never presume to become a sort of "secular church"—a claim it actually does have the presumption to make insofar as it wants to be *more* than a "mere" legal order. It is also characteristic of a state that the more it develops in the direction of the totalitarian state, the more hostile it becomes to the Church. Thus, the French republic was explicitly hostile to the Church because the republic *itself* wanted to educate its "citizens" in "civic virtues" (rather than let them be Christians with Christian virtues). Hitler's so-called Third Reich was hostile to the Church for the same reason. The people were to be educated in the national socialist worldview so that they would become National Socialists. The same goes for the Soviet Union. By state means, the people were to be educated as communists, that is, be brought to believe that the historical materialism of Marxism was the truth.

States, however, are not meant to be "worldview" communities (i.e., "churches"), but communities of *law*. Professional representatives of the human sciences (history, philosophy, theology, sociology) are in a much better position to judge the truth of historical materialism than are party leaders who have been elevated to become state authorities. If nonetheless these authorities should apply the apparatus of the state to the ends of the materialist worldview rather than to the ends of law, they are making a claim on behalf of the state to be a *church*. It matters not that such a "church" is a church of materialism. Whenever the spiritual church of Christianity is fought against, it is always a case of a striving towards *another* (i.e., opposing) "church."

⊕

The state may claim neither the authority and functions of the *church*, nor those of the *academy*. The state has no business deciding upon the truth of a scientific assertion, theory, or hypothesis, just as it has no call to decide on ethical, philosophical, theological, and mystical matters. For this reason, moreover, the state has no warrant to act as *educator*, for education has to do with worldview, ethics, and cultural formation. The pedagogical function does not belong *in any way* to what the state is authorized to undertake. Pedagogy is the common task of the church and of the academy. The state does indeed have to concern itself with the *external* conditions that the nature of education requires, but this can only be a matter of external relationships, never one of the content of education. The real function of the state is the function of *order*, of enforcing the law. Everything that exceeds this is an overreach of state power. The state is in no way an organization whose vocation is to rule, but one that is to serve. It is the ground beneath the feet of human beings, not the sky above their heads.

4

The *Problems* of International Law Today

n the period between the two Hague conferences and the present [1947], the whole Western
cultural community has had to undergo a series
of powerful shocks. The two world wars, the
Russian revolution, and the economic crisis of the 1930s
have faced humankind with problems on whose solution
the continued existence not only of international law, but of
culture *as such*, seem to depend. These problems cannot be
dealt with in their entirety within the framework of a treatise on the foundations of international law; they will,
therefore, form the object of a further study, which is conceived as a second part of the present treatise.[1] Here it is a
matter in particular of sketching the problems in their relation to the foundations of international law so that the
present state of international law can be viewed as a result of
historical experience.

Among the problems presented by historical experience,
not least by way of a series of catastrophes, the first is the
problem of the *world-organization*. Through the worldwide
dissemination of Western culture and the achievements of

[1] See page iii, note 7.

technology (along with the increased possibilities of commerce thus achieved), individual nations, and indeed the populations of all parts of the earth, have "come closer" to each other. If, according to Christian teaching, humanity was always a spiritually organic unity even before this, it is now not only a unity ideally or *in principle*, but also a unity in *fact*. The unity of humankind has become a fact. Indeed, culturally, politically, and economically, it represents a closely connected community with the same destiny, in which each member relies upon the other members. It follows from this, however, that, for example, the Monroe Doctrine of 1823, which envisages keeping Europe out of participation in the concerns of the American continent, and keeping America from meddling in European matters (isolationism), is shown to be an illusion. On the other hand, it will also be seen with absolute certainty that two opposed domains of legal order cannot lastingly exist alongside each other within the human community. In the long term, the international legal community can no longer permit itself "preserves" within the universal legal order that are ruled by force. The relationship of dictatorships to democracies, and the relationship of liberal, minimal states to totalitarian, maximal states *cannot*, in the long term, be regulated by means of demarcation. The nations of the earth have come too close to each other for there to be lines of demarcation; indeed, they will no longer *permit* themselves to be separated off in this way!

Thus the problem of a *world polity*, i.e., of the formation of a trans-state legal order embracing the whole of humankind, is closely connected to the problem of *meddling* in the internal affairs of individual states. A universal legal order has meaning or existence only if its principles obtain both for the "international law" domain of international commerce, and for "intra-state" law, i.e., the life of law within states. A state that recognizes principles as valid within international law but rejects them when it comes to its own internal affairs *cannot* in good faith act as a partner in the international legal community. Conversely, universal rights that *states* enjoy are worthless if they do not extend to the *individuals* within these states. If it is only the equal rights of *states* that are universally in force, without being accompanied by the universal validity of *human* rights, a paradoxical situation emerges in which human beings are obliged to champion rights *on behalf* of their states which they have themselves been *refused* by their states, and of which they have no knowledge from experience. How, for example, can a Soviet Russian subject argue *in good faith* for the freedom of the press and the freedom to demonstrate in relation to international commerce, if in his own country oral and written expressions of a view that contradicts the views of the *one* ruling party are punishable offences?

The task of establishing an effective world polity thus requires a system of organized, equal, and universal control of internal affairs. That is, it requires continual legal and legitimate *intervention*. However, the necessity of intervention brings with it an alteration in principle in the treatment of the problem of *sovereignty*. For intervention, as an acknowledged legal remedy, demands a re-evaluation of the absolute sovereignty of the state. It demands in particular a limitation of this principle. Just as there were once unlimitedly sovereign rulers, but then an age dawned in which the sovereignty of monarchs was gradually limited, so has historical development now reached the stage, in relation to states, at which unlimited sovereignty must give way to *lim-*

ited sovereignty. But the limitation of the state's sovereignty necessarily entails an increase in the significance and value of *individual persons*. At the Nuremberg trials, individual people were held to account for deeds carried out in the name of the state. For "the state is not an abstract entity. Its rights and duties are the rights and duties of men. Its actions are the actions of men."[2]

With this, the exclusive *legal subjecthood* of the state in international law is placed in question. And a further problem arises—the problem of the state's and the individual's capacity for law, for action, and for infringements of law, in the particular sense that, under international law, legal subjecthood ought also to be granted to the individual. This has become especially indispensable as a result of the concept of the commission of a *crime* under international law, a concept henceforth accepted into international legal practice, and distinguished from a mere *offence* under international law by the fact that the individual person who commits it can be punished. Thus, an unprovoked war of aggression is a crime under international law,[3] for which the *state* has to pay compensation (for the state, the war is thus merely an offence), whereas the responsible individuals are punishable as *criminals*.

Thus does *penal law* find its place in international law. Since the penal function is to be exercised by the international legal community, the problem of *obligatory arbitra-*

---

[2] From the speech for the prosecution made by the chief prosecutor at the Nuremberg trial, Sir Hartley Shawcross ("Die Gegenwart," 24–25, Freiburg, December 31, 1946).

[3] "Crime against peace," the first of the three points of the accusation at the Nuremberg trial.

tion (and thus also of the international *system of sanctions*) is a most timely one, for if war is henceforth to be prohibited as a means of rectifying international difficulties, then another means must be provided. This means can only be an international court of arbitration, a court that is to function not only as a court of arbitration but also as a court for both passing sentence *and* deciding on punishments. This court can only show itself to be effective, however, if the compulsory enforcement of its judgments and its binding jurisdiction are guaranteed by corresponding international instruments of power. A trans-state judiciary cannot exist without a trans-state executive. And neither are possible without a trans-state legislature, since the trans-state court must hold to trans-state norms (laws, treaties, declarations).

And so, the development of this complex of problems leads back to the main problem—to the *world polity* and, indeed, to the necessity for a *world state* equipped with these three powers. The League of Nations and the United Nations are steps along the path from a federation of states to a federated state with these three powers—these powers being a world legislature, a world executive, and a world judiciary.

⊕

Alongside these first-order problems of principle bound up with the world state, there are also in the present day a number of problems that have emerged from political practice and urgently demand a solution. For example, practice in recent decades has posed the problem of the international validity of elections and plebiscites. Previously, the principle in force was that election and referendum procedures were an internal matter of the state concerned. It was assumed that they would be carried out by the state concerned in a *bona fide* manner, precisely on the grounds that it was a state, and as such would act in public. The experience of elections and referendums in National Socialist Germany, in Fascist Italy, in the territories occupied by the Soviet Union (the Baltic republics of Estonia, Latvia, and Lithuania), in Poland, and in the Balkan states has, however, unequivocally demonstrated that elections and referendums that are significant for the international *status quo ante*[4] can be carried out by applying methods that make the results of popular referendums appear to represent the will of the state's government, when they do not. The juridical concept of the state's *dolus* (intention) finds a perfect application here. The assumption of good faith that had prevailed previously is thus shattered, and is invalid, at least as far as concerns those states that are not legal states in the sense of having a democratic constitution. From the assumption of the state's good faith having become invalid, and from the recognition of the possibility of the *dolus* on the state's side, there follows the problem of the international audit of referendums needed under international law.

To the practical problems of international law at the present time belongs also the problem of the *legal succession* in the state. For example, the Soviet Russian government has refused to honor the financial obligations of the previous Russian empire by claiming that the new socialist state was in no way a continuation of the previous monarchist, then democratic, state.[5] Conversely, the same Soviet government claimed (and claimed successfully) the earlier terri-

---

[4] The "not yet achieved" *status quo.* ED

[5] Russia was a democratic republic from March to November 1917.

tories of Tsarist Russia, including the Baltic republics, eastern Poland, Bessarabia; and even the Far-Eastern lands Russia had been obliged to cede to Japan in 1905: Port Arthur and South Sakhalin. Is Soviet Russia, then, a legal successor to the Tsarist government and to that of democratic Russia from the time of the Kerensky regime? If not, it has no legal title to the lands it has incorporated into its territory. Their incorporation would therefore show itself to be mere imperialism, a naked act of power. Moreover, if the Soviet government *is* the legal successor to the November revolution of 1917, it ought to own not only the claims of its legal predecessor, but also its obligations.

Are the territory and the people the only criteria for the succession to a state? Or is the government (the internal legal and social order) the decisive factor in determining whether the succession has taken place or not? For the peoples of eastern Poland and the Baltic republics (including those of Russian origin among them), Soviet Russia was decidedly *not* the successor to the previous Russia, any more than it was the successor to the border states that had come into being out of the previous Russia. For this reason, the plebiscites in eastern Poland and the Baltic republics should not be about unification with *Russia*, but about solidarity or non-solidarity with the communist political and social *system*—and, indeed, with the worldview of historical materialism. In reality, therefore, for these nations it is not a question of "re-unification with Russia" (which may have quite a number of supporters) but of their incorporation into the part of the world ruled by communism. The "abducted persons" from the Baltic republics and from eastern Poland who are today [1947] staying in camps in Germany, are not refusing to return to their "homeland." They are refusing to exchange the world of democratic freedoms for the world of the totalitarian communist dictatorship. Their "homeland," to which they do not return, no longer exists. True, the same territory and a portion of the same people exist, but the cultural, political, and economic life of their former homeland has in the meantime become the opposite of what they knew as a homeland.

Thus, the question arises whether the *people* suffices to determine the identity of a state, the succession to a state, and the membership of the state. Are Russian emigrants, for example, "Russians" in the sense of having a connection of some kind with present-day Soviet Russia? If they are not (for this is how the question has been settled in practice, by describing them as "stateless"), this is because they have decided for the legal order that rules in the rest of the world. They are citizens of this legal community, and should be recognized as such, and not considered simply as "stateless."

⊕

These and similar questions face international law today. They are not merely theoretical questions, but questions upon which the fate of millions of living human beings depends. International law today faces important tasks, and an absolutely immense responsibility. It will not be able to do its job, however, if it does not reflect upon its true historical, legal, ethical, philosophical, and religious *foundations*, so that, as a result of clarity about matters of principle gained from this process of reflection, it can then turn to the regulation of the factual state of affairs. In the present study, an attempt has been made to reflect in this way on the historical, legal, ethical, philosophical, and religious foundations of international law. In a further study, conceived as a continuation of the present one, an attempt will be made to demonstrate the *applicability* of the principles, as they have been sketched in this concluding chapter, to the international legal problems of the present.[6]

[6] See page iii, note 7.

www.ingramcontent.com/pod-product-compliance
Lightning Source LLC
Chambersburg PA
CBHW022008080426
42733CB00007B/522

* 9 7 8 1 6 2 1 3 8 9 3 1 6 *